Donated by...

The

Jost-Ore

THE LETTERS OF
D. H. LAWRENCE
& AMY LOWELL
1914 ~ 1925

EDITED BY
E. CLAIRE HEALEY
& KEITH CUSHMAN

BLACK SPARROW PRESS
SANTA BARBARA ~ ~ 1985

For the Lawrence side of the correspondence we gratefully acknowledge the permission of the Estate of the late Mrs. Frieda Lawrence Ravagli, Laurence Pollinger Ltd., and Viking Penguin, Inc. We also gratefully acknowledge the permission of the Cambridge University Press.

For the Lowell side of the correspondence we gratefully acknowledge the permission of G. d'Andelot Belin and Brinton P. Roberts, Trustees under the Will of Amy Lowell. This correspondence is printed by permission of the Houghton Library.

Library of Congress Cataloging-in-Publication Data
Lawrence, D.H. (David Herbert), 1885–1930.
  The letters of D.H. Lawrence & Amy Lowell, 1914–1925.

  1. Lawrence, D.H. (David Herbert), 1885–1930—
Correspondence. 2. Lowell, Amy, 1874–1925—Correspondence.
3. Authors, English—20th century—Correspondence.
4. Poets, American—20th century—Correspondence.
I. Lowell, Amy, 1874–1925.   II. Healey, E. Claire.
III. Cushman, Keith.   IV. Title
PR6023.A93Z5336   1985   823'.912   85-15087
ISBN 0-87685-667-9
ISBN 0-87685-668-7 (deluxe)

Editorial Note

Lawrence wrote his letters to Lowell by hand, but Lowell's replies were typed by a secretary. Consequently we have treated the two sides of the correspondence slightly differently. We have attempted to present the texts of Lawrence's letters verbatim, including eccentricities of spelling, punctuation, capitalization, and paragraphing. In contrast we have silently corrected the few typographical errors in Lowell's letters. We have let stand mistakes in Lowell's letters that do not seem typographical (for example, Sennor for Zennor and Wicksworth for Wirksworth). We have slightly regularized Lawrence's headings. Postscripts have been moved to a position after the signature no matter where they are found in the manuscripts.

The few letters between Frieda Lawrence and Amy Lowell are printed at the end of the correspondence between Lawrence and Lowell. Explanatory notes are located at the end of the volume so that they will not intrude upon the flow of the letters.

Introduction

The friendship between D. H. Lawrence and Amy Lowell began as a chapter in the history of Imagism. In the summer of 1914 Lowell traveled to England with Ada Russell, the former actress who had just agreed to become her companion. Lowell was looking for Keats materials for her collection and for the biography she was planning. She wanted to arrange for English publication of her second book of poetry, *Sword Blades and Poppy Seed,* and to place individual poems with magazine editors. Always the shrewd businesswoman and promoter of poetry, she persuaded Macmillan of London to accept an arrangement in which they would distribute 100 copies of *Sword Blades* for only 10% of the retail price, with the other 90% to go to Lowell. And Lowell was anxious to meet Ezra Pound and become a more influential member of the Imagist group. Pound's anthology, *Des Imagistes,* including one poem by Amy Lowell, had been published in February.

By this time Pound was feeling that the Imagist program was too limited and was moving on to his association with Vorticism. Nevertheless, he resented the intrusion of this wealthy, energetic, dominating fellow American. On 17 July Lowell held a dinner at the Dieu-donné Restaurant in honor of *Des Imagistes,* attended by a number of the contributors. But throughout the occasion Pound .

> rebuffed her attempts at seriousness with ill-bred, impertinent levity. In answer to her question about a precise formula for *Imagisme,* he left the table and came back in a few minutes wearing an old-fashioned tin tub on his head in caricature of a helmet of some knight-errant. He produced hilarious laughter, in which Amy joined, but hers was a hard and hurt laugh.[1]

A clash between Pound and Lowell was surely inevitable, both for temperamental and aesthetic reasons. Such poets as Richard Aldington, his wife Hilda Doolittle (H.D.), and F. S. Flint already felt "fed up with Ezra."[2] Lowell was ambitious, and she had the organizational capacity and financial means to make something happen in the literary world.

On 30 July 1914 Lowell held another dinner, this time in her suite in the top floor of the Berkeley Hotel. She invited the

Aldingtons and the American poet John Gould Fletcher. The guests of honor were D. H. Lawrence and his wife Frieda, who, like the Aldingtons, were only recently married. Lowell knew Lawrence's work from his contributions to *Poetry* and through Pound's favorable review of his *Love Poems* in July 1913. She considered Lawrence one of the best young English writers. Lowell was also toying with the idea of editing a review of her own. Dinner at the Berkeley was a great success, from the

> moment the door opened, and a tall slim young man, with bright red hair and the most brilliant blue eyes, came in with a lithe, springing step. . . .
>
> As guest of honour Lawrence sat next to Amy, and they made a curious contrast, if only because one was so lean and the other so plump. Probably Fletcher and H.D. appreciated more than I did the spectacle of the coal miner's son sitting at the right hand of a Lowell. . . .
>
> Amy came out well that evening. There was not a trace of condescension in her and she did a difficult thing well—she expressed her warm admiration for Lawrence's work without flattery or insincerity and without embarrassing him.[3]

The next day Lawrence wrote Harriet Monroe about the dinner, complaining that "when I see all the understanding and suffering and the pure intelligence necessary for the simple perceiving of poetry, then I know it is an almost hopeless business to publish the stuff at all. . . ."[4] But Lowell had already recruited him for a new publishing venture.

Lowell's break with Pound came over her plan to bring out an annual anthology of new Imagist poetry. This was the great period for anthologies. Lowell's primary inspiration was the extremely successful *Georgian Poetry. Some Imagist Poets* appeared in 1915, 1916, and 1917 featuring the same group of six poets: Lowell, Lawrence, the Aldingtons, Fletcher, and Flint. The poems published were to be decided upon, at least in principle, jointly by all six contributors, and the profits were to be shared equally.

Meanwhile Pound perceived that Imagism would not be the same once Amy Lowell had gotten hold of it. "The hard, sharp edges of Pound's verse become blurred in Lowell's verse, and the nondiscursive Image becomes discursive. The territorial boundaries of the Image are no longer so carefully observed."[5] Pound insisted that Imagism stood for "hard light, clear edges" and could "not trust any democratized committee to maintain that standard."[6] Lowell's poetry was "the fluid, fruity, facile stuff we most wanted to avoid."[7]

Lawrence told Lowell that he wasn't an Imagist, and later in his life he even said that there had been no such thing as Imagism. But in July 1914 Lowell was undaunted, and Lawrence didn't mind publishing with Lowell's Imagists. Pound would insist that Lawrence "was an *Amygist*" rather than an Imagist; Lawrence never "accepted the Imagist program."[8] Certainly it is curious that Lawrence appeared at the same time in Imagist and Georgian anthologies. But as Aldington remembered, "Lawrence was such an individualist that he didn't care a hoot about groups and their alleged principles."[9]

The Imagist alliance formed by Lowell and Lawrence has more to do with the history of literary politics than the history of literature. The coteries and factions so characteristic of these years may have helped Lawrence discover his own voice, but he was more interested in these groups as a way to get his voice heard. From the beginning he brought to his art a fierce independence. Nor did Lowell recruit Lawrence to the Imagist cause for reasons of literary theory. Her own idea of Imagism was hazy and miscellaneous enough. Instead she truly admired Lawrence's poetry, and she realized that he was developing a critical reputation. Here was clearly a genius, a writer destined for greatness. By helping to foster his talent, Lowell would be advancing the cause of the new poetry, and she would also be advancing her own ambition to be a leader of that cause.

During the summer of 1914 Lawrence dined with Lowell at the Berkeley Hotel again. Another day Lowell and Ada Russell motored out to Buckinghamshire to spend the day with the Lawrences at the small cottage they were renting. After that summer in England, Lawrence and Lowell never met again, though they made an attempt in America in the summer of 1923. Nevertheless, they wrote each other for the ten years of life remaining to Lowell before her death in May 1925. During this decade Lowell was as prominent a literary figure as Lawrence. She enjoyed great critical esteem, high public visibility, and a wide audience. Interestingly, Lawrence was by far the more faithful correspondent. Of the eighty-four letters they wrote each other that survive, fifty-three are from Lawrence to Lowell, thirty-one from Lowell to Lawrence.[10]

Part of the fascination of the Lawrence-Lowell letters is the fact that both sides of the correspondence are still in existence. This is unusual among Lawrence's many correspondences, especially non-business correspondences, for he traveled light and did not save letters. However, it is not at all unusual among Lowell's correspondences. She was systematic in her ambition to be remembered by posterity, and she had the financial means to insure that the Amy Lowell archive would be well preserved and well organized. Lawrence's letters are among the many Lowell papers preserved in the Houghton Library at Harvard. The Lowell side of the correspondence survives at Harvard in carbon copies of Lowell's letters to Lawrence, typed by secretaries. The fluid, nonstop quality of many of Lowell's sentences suggests that it was her habit to dictate her letters.

Many of the letters have appeared in print before but only in a scattered fashion and often in incomplete texts. The great sourcebook for information about Lowell's life is S. Foster Damon's cumbersome *Amy Lowell: A Chronicle*, published in 1935, ten years after Lowell's death. Damon knew Lowell well from 1916 onward and was something of a disciple. He quotes regularly from the Lawrence-Lowell correspondence in his *Chronicle* as the letters "are of great literary value, and as Mr. Aldous Huxley overlooked them in editing Lawrence's *Collected Letters*."[11] (Huxley's edition of Lawrence's letters, published in 1932, is actually entitled *The Letters of D. H. Lawrence*.) Damon rarely prints a complete text. Harry T. Moore includes only four of Lawrence's letters to Lowell in his two-volume *Collected Letters*, published in 1962. He does cite other letters in his biography of Lawrence, *The Intelligent Heart* (1954, revised in 1974 as *The Priest of Love*). Lawrence–Lowell letters appear in the Nehls *Composite Biography*, and Paul Delany quotes from the Lawrence side of the correspondence in *D. H. Lawrence's Nightmare* (1978), his account of the war years. Eventually the Cambridge University Press will have published all of Lawrence's letters to Lowell, but to date only the first three volumes, through early June 1921, have appeared. Many errors are to be found in the previous printings of these letters, including a number in the Cambridge edition.[12] Few of Lowell's letters to Lawrence have been published, and of course no previous attempt has been made to publish a complete edition of both sides of the correspondence.

Needless to say, Lawrence and Lowell add up to a marvelously assorted pair. While Lawrence was born into the family of a Midlands coal miner, the Lowells of Boston were among the most substantial of Brahmins. Lowell's brother Percival, an astronomer, founded the Lowell Observatory in Flagstaff and predicted the existence of Pluto years before its discovery. Her brother Lawrence was President of Harvard during a quarter of a century of major academic growth. Amy Lowell's mother was actually a Boston Lawrence, but if Lawrence and Lowell were somehow remotely related, it wasn't discernible.

Self-interest was part of the relationship for both writers. Lawrence realized the value of having an influential, wealthy friend at the center of the new poetry in the United States. As noted previously, it was a personal coup for Lowell to be able to enlist Lawrence under the banner of her version of Imagism. Yet it was not self-interest that kept the correspondence going. Instead the letters were generated primarily out of a bona fide, enduring (though not deep) friendship.

Amy Lowell was a force to be reckoned with, but there were invisible scars. As a child she had been an ugly duckling, but she did not grow up to become a beautiful swan. She also felt neglected as the baby of the Augustus Lowell clan. Amy was nineteen years younger than her brother Percival, seventeen-and-a-half years younger than her brother Lawrence. She had two older sisters, but the younger of the two was already twelve when Amy was born. She was awkward, plain, plump, and lonely, not at all the right material for the Boston debutante set. She came to poetry late, publishing her first collection, *A Dome of Many-Coloured Glass*, in 1912 when she was thirty-eight. As she became respected as a poet and important as an advocate of the new poetry, she also became prominent as a character and eccentric in the popular press. Amy Lowell was the proper Bostonian manquée, broad of girth, strong-willed, energetic, and aggressive. She smoked light Manila cigars, and she lived with a woman. She was imposing and demanding, but she was also vulnerable.

The "tall slim young man, with bright red hair and the most brilliant blue eyes" who "came in with a lithe, springing step" that evening in London made a lasting impression on Lowell. But the ensuing relationship depended on the fact that the remarkably intuitive Lawrence perceived the wounded, emotionally needy woman beneath Lowell's aggressive, domineering, born-to-command manner. She found in Lawrence a gifted poet who would join with her and her fellow poets in the three annual editions of *Some Imagist Poets*. But she also found a graceful friend whose sympathetic interest provided some of the approbation she so deeply craved. Lowell was talking about poetry when she told Lawrence, "I do not know any one whom I would rather please than you" (Letter 65). But her words reverberate.

Lowell was especially grateful for the way Lawrence penetrated her poses, especially her poetic poses. His criticism of her books as she sent them to him is characteristic of his criticism of his friends' writings, always both forthright and tactful. He warned her at the beginning that he would be "prowling through [her] verses like a beast of prey" (Letter 6). Above all he counseled her to be herself in her poetry rather than hiding behind brightly colored technique or fashionable French mannerisms or *japanoiserie*. "Why go to France or anywhere else for your inspiration," he wrote. "If it doesn't come out of your own heart, real Amy Lowell, it is no good" (Letter 7). She valued this criticism highly, not only because she found it perceptive but also because it spoke directly to her sense of her real self. Poetry was itself a bond between Lawrence and Lowell.

Nevertheless, an unpleasant undercurrent surfaces periodically. If Lowell was emotionally needy, Lawrence was financially needy, especially during World War I. Lowell sent him a used typewriter in the autumn of 1914 (he loved it), and she also sent money from time to time, at least once in response to an embarrassing begging letter from Frieda (Letter 89). He loathed being the "charity-boy of literature" (Letter 49), and he hated to receive the money he badly needed. Lawrence rendered thanks to Lowell by dedicating *New Poems* to her. Originally he had suggested that he dedicate *Studies in Classic American Literature* to her. The dedication he proposed, apparently in some seriousness, reveals his complex attitude toward his patroness:

> To
> Amy Lowell
> Who buttered my bread
> These few fair words.
> For she can butter her own parsnips.
> Being well-to-do
> She gave to the thankless
> Because she thought it was worth it.
>
> (Letter 27)

The actual dedication of *New Poems* is simply "To Amy Lowell." Lawrence refused to be beholden to the rich and powerful of the world, and Amy Lowell was one of the rich and powerful. He advised his friend and agent Mountsier in March 1921 "*not* to be too humble with editors, publishers, Amys or any other stinkers with money or office."[13]

There was also the question of Lawrence's desire to come to America and to become more established in the American market.

Early in 1916 Lowell told Lawrence that he would find America "a stimulating place to live and work in" (Letter 15), but she changed her tune once it seemed he might actually come. When Lawrence asked Lowell in May 1919 if she, as "the only person I know, actually, in America," could "help me a bit to find my feet when I come" (Letter 42), she answered emphatically and at great length that it was a mistake for him to come to Boston or indeed America. She added in August that "I cannot have people stay in the house with me," for "it makes me very nervous to have guests" (Letter 45). The same day she repeated her anxieties in a separate letter to Frieda. At this point Lowell obviously felt comfortable being Lawrence's friend only from a safe distance. Lawrence, the author of a banned novel, had achieved widespread notoriety. Despite her cigars, her female companion, and her championing of innovative poetry, Lowell was much more a Brahmin than a bohemian. No doubt she also feared getting stuck with Lawrence once he was in the States. But despite this aggressive rebuff, Lawrence maintained his poise and courtesy. From Florence he wrote in November, "I have not thanked you for your letters, which were really kind, and which I understood" (Letter 47). Though he traveled all over the world, he kept the correspondence going.

In late November 1920 Lawrence wrote Lowell that he would send her the manuscript of *Birds, Beasts and Flowers* "for your opinion, am so curious to know" (Letter 59). He was not aware that Lowell had undergone her third hernia operation just a month before. As Lawrence waited for Lowell to return the manuscript, he grew more and more choleric in letters to Mountsier. Late in January Lowell was a "good soul," but a month later she was a "bitch." In early March Lawrence cruelly remarked that Lowell was "trying to keep afloat on the gas of her own importance: hard work, considering her bulk." He was ready to "send her to blazes, along with her cigars."[14] But when Lawrence learned the reason for the long delay, he immediately wrote Lowell (the letter has been lost) and asked her to buy a pot of fuchsias with his share of the latest installment of royalties from *Some Imagist Poets*.

Lowell was an early advocate of Lawrence's writings in America, both in print and in her lectures, appreciating his power and originality. In a review of *Look! We Have Come Through!* she wrote, "Sincere, loyal, serious, strong, permeated with beauty, scored upon by tragedy, he is himself and no other. We may like him or dislike him, but we cannot ignore him if we would know the full circle of English poetry to-day." She also admired the "stark and rather terrible power" of *Sons and Lovers*. But the same power that attracted her to Lawrence's writings also troubled her. Lawrence was "an excessively sensitive man, things hurt him profoundly, he is raw from contacts which have excoriated his soul." The weakness of *Look! We Have Come Through!* is that "art is not raw fact. . . . The volume fails by a too loud insistence upon one thing, by an almost neurotic beating, beating, upon the same tortured note."[15] More candidly, she wrote H.D. that Lawrence "is getting cracked on sex things, and his presentation of them is not always of the most refined."[16]

Lowell defends Lawrence by attempting to spiritualize him. If he is "a poet of sensation," that sensation must be "the bodily efflorescence of a spiritual growth." Desire in Lawrence is but the "outward and visible form of an inward and spiritual grace."[17] In the correspondence she advises him to be "a little more reticent on this one subject" and to "simply use an India rubber in certain places, and then you can come into your own" (Letter 36). In warning him not to come to America she remarks that "the erotic side of your work has been too greatly stressed here." Lowell says that this is a case of misperception: one can imagine Lawrence's sardonic laughter when he read that actually "there exists no more high-minded nor fine character in literature" (Letter 43). Lowell seems to be making Lawrence over into a closet Boston Brahmin. Actually most of his artistic career was dedicated to the destruction of high-mindedness. No wonder he asked, "Are you shy of me?" (Letter 42). He also must have been appalled by Lowell's unabashed careerism.

Lawrence's own literary taste was extremely eclectic, but often when he praises Lowell's writings he seems to be straining to accentuate the positive, trying to find something good to say to balance his criticisms. In November 1916 after receiving *Men, Women and Ghosts* he writes Lowell that he prefers the book to *Sword Blades and Poppy Seeds* and he scrupulously picks out the individual poems he likes best. But the next month he writes A. W. McLeod that Lowell—whom he identifies as James Russell Lowell's daughter!—is "not a good poetess," but he calls her "a very good friend."[18] For good friends he found good things to say. Sometimes, however, Lawrence manages unfeigned enthusiasm. Once he even suggests—bizarrely enough—that they would do well to collaborate on a play.

Lawrence and Lowell came closest to meeting again in July and August of 1923 when Lawrence and Frieda spent nearly a month in the New York City area. Failures of communication, a dental appointment, "a thousand and one things to do" (Letter 81), a "catenation of circumstances" (Letter 82) prevented another meeting. Lawrence was embarrassed that he and Frieda hadn't succeeded in getting to Boston after years of protesting that he hoped they would meet again. However, though he couldn't get to Boston, he did spend four days in Buffalo visiting Bessie Freeman before proceeding to Los Angeles. Lawrence and Lowell both expressed their regrets that their meeting did not come to pass, yet both also seemed somewhat relieved. Perhaps Lawrence had not altogether forgotten Lowell's remark that it made her "very nervous to have guests." Perhaps after nine years they were both apprehensive about whether a relationship that worked via the mails could be resumed in person.

Another nasty remark about Lowell shows up in a letter Lawrence wrote his publisher Thomas Seltzer in September 1922: "Amy is just a cupboard that loves itself. I'm glad that by sheer intuition I gave her a few slaps last time I wrote her. She goes off my list now."[19] But she never did go off the list of friends and acquaintances he periodically corresponded with. Lawrence wrote his last letter to Lowell just five weeks before her death.

The D. H. Lawrence–Amy Lowell letters are not finally a great correspondence. It didn't help that the two writers never again met after the summer of 1914. The literary talk contained in the letters is not consistently of a high order, even at the beginning.[20] When it comes to literature, Lowell writes almost exclusively about politics and the literary market-place.

Still, there is something touching about the "odd congenital understanding" (Letter 49) that endured between this unlikely literary pair, both destined for early deaths. The correspondence meant very much to Lowell, and Lawrence cared enough about it to keep it going. As Lawrence wrote Lowell less than a year before she died, "we'll keep a bit of decent kindliness at the bottom of our hearts" (Letter 83). That bit of kindliness — along with unstinting warmth and sympathy — irradiates the correspondence. The Lawrence–Lowell letters survive as rewarding human documents as well as instructive souvenirs of a rich period in modern literary history.

Notes

1 Jean Gould, *Amy: The World of Amy Lowell and the Imagist Movement* (New York: Dodd, Mead, 1975), p. 128.

2 Richard Aldington, *Life for Life's Sake: A Book of Reminiscences* (New York: Viking, 1941), p. 139.

3 Aldington, p. 141.

4 D. H. Lawrence, *The Letters of D. H. Lawrence*, Volume II, ed. George J. Zytaruk and James T. Boulton (Cambridge: Cambridge University Press, 1981), p. 203.

5 Kim A. Herzinger, *D. H. Lawrence in His Time: 1908-1915* (Lewisburg, Pa.: Bucknell University Press, 1982), p. 149.

6 Ezra Pound, *The Letters of Ezra Pound, 1907-1941*, ed. D. D. Paige (New York: Harcourt, 1950), p. 38.

7 Aldington, p. 137.

8 Pound, p. 212.

9 Aldington, p. 140.

10 One letter is from Ada Russell to Lawrence and two from unspecified secretaries. The Frieda Lawrence–Amy Lowell correspondence, five letters from Frieda and one from Lowell, is printed after the Lawrence–Lowell letters. The Frieda–Lowell letters are numbered 88-93.

11 S. Foster Damon, *Amy Lowell: A Chronicle* (Boston: Houghton, 1935), p. xviii.

12 The Cambridge text of Lawrence's letter of 22 August 1914 has the following errors on page 209 of Volume II: Referring to "Ballad of Another Ophelia," Cambridge has Lawrence saying "put it in as you love me." Actually he says, "put it in an you love me," using a regionalism for "if." Cambridge has "The MS. poems I sent you here have not been published, yes." The correct reading is "The MS. poems I sent you here have not been published. Yes." The third error on this page is "Don't lose MS—of the 'Irises' poem." "MS—" should be "MS." In the letter of 16 October 1914, p. 224, Cambridge prints "sehr-ge-ehrrte" instead of Lawrence's correct "sehr-ge-ehrte." In the letter of 18 December 1914, p. 244, Cambridge substitutes "conservation" for "conversation."

There are also a number of definite misreadings in Volume III of the Cambridge edition. In the letter of 14 November 1916, p. 31, it should be "the lacquer music-stand," not "the lacquer music-stands." (A brief glance at Lowell's poem, which features only one music-stand, could have cleared up any doubt about this reading.) In the letter of 5 November 1918, p. 296, Cambridge prints "Que n'importe" for the correct "Que m'importe," and in the bargain the editors choose not to translate the phrase in a footnote.

16

In the letter of 5 April 1919, p. 347, the Cambridge reading is the garbled "I had Flu. also—" although Lawrence has clearly written "I had Flu—also—" Similarly in the letter of 3 July 1919, p. 369, "quite soon—The wind blows that way." should be "quite soon. The wind blows that way." In the letter of 26 June 1920, p. 557, Cambridge prints "Ciccio's rich," but Lawrence has written "Ciccio is rich." All textual editors realize that perfection is to be striven for rather than achieved.

[13] D. H. Lawrence, *The Letters of D. H. Lawrence*, Volume III, ed. James T. Boulton and Andrew Robertson (Cambridge: Cambridge University Press, 1984), p. 684.

[14] *The Letters of D. H. Lawrence*, Volume III, ed. Boulton and Robertson, pp. 653, 673, 677.

[15] Amy Lowell, *Poetry and Poets*, ed. Ferris Greenslet (Boston: Houghton, 1930), pp. 174, 175, 177, 173.

[16] Letter from Lowell to Hilda Doolittle, 23 November 1915, in the Houghton Library, Harvard University.

[17] *Poetry and Poets*, pp. 164, 164-5.

[18] *The Letters of D. H. Lawrence*, Volume III, ed. Boulton and Robertson, p. 61.

[19] D. H. Lawrence, *Letters to Thomas and Adele Seltzer*, ed. Gerald M. Lacy (Santa Barbara: Black Sparrow, 1976), p. 41.

[20] One exception is Lawrence's lengthy discussion of Lowell's *Men, Women and Ghosts* on 14 November 1916. This letter is an acute criticism of Lowell's poetry, but it is even more interesting for what it shows about Lawrence's thinking as he struggled with *Women in Love*.

The Letters of
D. H. Lawrence
&
Amy Lowell
1914—1925

Illustrations follow page 82.

1

9 Selwood Terrace
South Kensington, SW
Sunday.
[9 August 1914]

Dear Miss Lowell,

I am back in London for a week or so. Will you ask my wife and me to come & see you—we should like very much to do so. And will you give the Aldingtons[1] our address—of course I've forgotten theirs—and tell them we should like to come to tea. I am occupied Tuesday & Wednesday afternoons, but otherwise we are free.

Please forgive the pencil—there is no pen & ink in the house. And we are so miserable about the war. My wife is German, so you may imagine—her father was an army officer. Everything seems gone to pieces.

Yours Very Sincerely

D. H. Lawrence

2

9, Selwood Terrace,
South Kensington, S. W.
11 August 1914

My Dear Miss Lowell,

It is very good & nice of you to ask us to dinner on Thursday. We look forward very much to coming. I suppose I needn't dress— just as you ordain. Is Mrs Russell staying with you?—I did not know.[2] My respects to her, and it is a pleasure to meet her again.

All my wails & laments I shall pour out when I come.

Küss die Hand

D. H. Lawrence

21

3

The Triangle
Bellingdon Lane
Chesham
Bucks.
22 Aug 1914

Dear Miss Lowell,

Here we are settled in our cottage, which is really very nice. I spend my days whitewashing the upper rooms, having a rare old time. Meanwhile I grind over in my soul the war news. Germany is a queer country: one can't regard it dispassionately. I alternate between hating it thoroughly, stick stock & stone, and yearning over it fit to break my heart. I cant help feeling it a young and adorable country—adolescent—with the faults of adolescence. There is no peace during this war. But I must say, my chief grief & misery is for Germany—so far.

In the poetry book, for my seven, will you please put

1. Ballad of Another Ophelia—beginning "O the green glimmer of apples in the orchard." Harriett Monroe[3] has got it, & wants to publish the far end of it & leave out the first half: see her in blazes. But even if you don't like the poem, please put it in an you love me.

2. Illicit—beginning—I've forgotten—something about "a faint, lost ribbon of rainbow." It is in "Poetry."

3. The Youth Mowing—also in "Poetry."

4. "Birthday"—also in Poetry—"If I were well-to-do"

5. Isar Rose Poems.

6. Tired of the Boat. } MS. enclosed

7. Scent of Irises

This is very roughly my selection. I'm quite amenable to change. Tell me yours, & let us compromise.[4] The MS. poems I sent you here have not been published. Yes, Tired of the Boat, two years ago in the English Review—in an unrevised version. Don't lose MS. of the Irises poem, will you?—it is the only copy. I can't be bothered to write it out again. You might, if you like, offer these poems to Harriett Monroe: but not unless you like. I only insist on your taking the Ballad of Another Ophelia.

Can't you come & see us? Can't you drive out here in your motor car—about 30 miles. Come to Chesham, through Harrow. In

Chesham ask for Elliotts farm at Bellingdon—we are 100 yards from the farm. We should be delighted to see you. Do try to come—any day, at any hour—you will eat eggs if there is nothing else in the house—& cheese & milk & bacon—perfectly rural & idyllic.

When you go to America, please abuse Mitchell Kennerley for me, & *please* make him send me some money. He owes me some, even if it were no more than the bad cheque for £10 he sent me & I sent back.[5] Won't you drive over for the day, with Mrs Russell or the Aldingtons?

My wife & I send many regards to you & to Mrs Russell.

Yours

D. H. Lawrence

4

The Triangle
Bellingdon Lane
Chesham
Bucks
Tuesday
[25 August 1914]

Dear Miss Lowell,

What good news, to hear that you will come and see us. We shall look out for you on Thursday afternoon. Ask for Elliotts farm, Bellingdon, when you get to Chesham.

Tante belle cose from us to you & Mrs Russell.

D. H. Lawrence

5

The Triangle
Bellingdon Lane
Chesham
Bucks
18 Sept 1914.

Dear Miss Lowell,

I suppose by now you are at home with your dogs & your manuscripts.[6] Here it is raining, & the apples blown down lie almost like green lights in the grass. Kennst du das Land, wo die Citronen blühen?[7] Yes, so do I. But now I hear the rain-water trickling animatedly into the green and rotten water-butt.

Will you send me the poems of mine that you think of including in the anthology, so that I can go over them and make any improvements I am capable of.

You won't forget to go to Mitchell Kennerley for me, will you? My agent[8] writes me that he also fails utterly to rouse any echo of response from that gentleman in New York. Tell him about the £25 cheque promised, & the £10 non-valid cheque that came and returned to him, bad penny as it was. Tell him how the hollow of his silence gets bigger & bigger, till he becomes almost a myth. Ask him if he received the MS. of my novel.[9] And I kiss your hand, dear Miss Lowell, for being so good to me.

We are likely to stay in this cottage till I am a silvery haired old gentleman going round patting the curly polls of the cottage toddlers. Nobody will pay me any money, and nobody is good to me, and already the robins are brightening to sing, and the holly berries on the hedges are getting redder. Ahimé—ahimé![10] It's winter, and the wooden gate is black and sodden in the rain, above the raw, cold puddles. Ahimé once more. Im dunklen Laub die gold Orangen glühn.[11] Give our very warm regards to your friend, & to you

tante belle cose

D. H. Lawrence

My wife sends her love to you.

We've made some first rate blackberry jelly. That's my nearest approach to poetry here.

6

Dear Miss Lowell,

Over the type-writer I have got quite tipsy with joy: a frightfully heady bit of news.[12] Already my wife & I are pushing each other off the chair and fighting as to who shall work it—the type-writer, I mean. I wonder when it will come: I wonder if it is already on the Atlantic: I wonder if it will be small enough for me to smuggle into Italy. I shall cherish it like a jewel. I always say that my only bit of property in the world is a silver watch—which is true. Now my realm is a type writer: I am a man of property: I feel quite scared lest I shall have incurred new troubles & new responsibilities.—But I hope it won't be very long in coming—the type writer—not the trouble—unberufen, unberufen.[13]

By the same post has come a cheque for £50, a grant to me from the Royal Literary Fund.[14] But that bores me. There is no joy in their tame thin-gutted charity. I would fillip it back at their old noses, the stodgy, stomachy authors, if I could afford it. But I can't.

We are also curiously awaiting your book of poems.[15] You'll see me prowling through your verses like a beast of prey: and oh, the hyaena howl I shall send up when I seize on a lameness. You wait.

But for the Lord's sake, don't be modest, & say you'll listen to me. Disclaim me to start with, or I won't say anything at all.

And don't talk about putting me in the safe with Keats and Shelley. It scares me out of my life, like the disciples at the Transfiguration. But I'd like to know Coleridge, when Chaaron has rowed me over.

It is good of you to see Kennerley. I don't want him ever to publish me anything ever any more as long as either of us lives. So you can say what you like to him. But I think that really he is rather nice. Just ask him about my things, will you:—no more. Pinker, my agent, is anxious to get me free from him, as there is an American publisher wants to make terms with Pinker for me.

But I should be very glad of the short story arrangement, if Kennerley is off. I am having a book of stories published shortly by Duckworth. It will be called "The Prussian Officer & other Stories," because it begins with that story I called "Honor & Arms": which, by the way, is sold to the Metropolitan Magazine, in America. Also these stories need not go through my agent. If Houghton would correspond with Duckworth, at 3 Henrietta St. Covent Garden—& if the Kennerley arrangement were off, then the thing could be settled most beautifully.[16]

We have had a beautiful dim autumn, of pale blue atmosphere & white stubble and hedges hesitating to change. But I've been seedy, and I've grown a red beard, behind which I shall take as much cover henceforth as I can, like a creature under a bush. My dear God, I've been miserable this autumn, enough to turn into wood, and be a graven image of myself.

I wish myself we could come in and drink wine and laugh with you, and hear some of other people's music. When I'm rich I shall come to America.

We may go back to Italy at the very end of the year, if we can get, & if I can get in a little more money, which of course I shall. Greet Mrs Russell from us. I can feel her good will towards us very real over there.

Viele herzliche Grüsse, sehr-ge-ehrte Frau[17]

D. H. Lawrence

7

Bellingdon Lane
Chesham
Bucks
18 Nov 1914

Dear Amy Lowell,

The type-writer has come, and is splendid. Why did you give it away?—I am sure you must have wanted to keep it. But it goes like a bubbling pot, frightfully jolly. My wife sits at it fascinated, patiently spelling out, at this moment, my war poem.

Oh—the War Number of "Poetry" came—I thought it pretty bad. The war-atmosphere has blackened here—it is soaking in, and getting more like part of our daily life, and therefore much grimmer. So I was quite cross with you for writing about bohemian glass and stalks of flame, when the thing is so ugly and bitter to the soul.[18]

I like *you* in your poetry. I don't believe in affecting France.[19] I like you when you are straight out. I really liked very much The Precinct, Rochester. There you had a sunny, vivid, intensely still atmosphere that was very true. I dont like your first long poem a bit. I think "A Taxi" is very clever and futuristic — and good. I like the one about the dog looking [in] the window — good.[20]

Why don't you always be yourself. Why go to France or anywhere else for your inspiration. If it doesn't come out of your own heart, real Amy Lowell, it is no good, however many colours it may have. I wish one saw more of your genuine strong, sound self in this book, full of common-sense & kindness and the restrained, almost bitter, Puritan passion. Why do you deny the bitterness in your nature, when you write poetry? Why do you take a pose? It causes you always to shirk your issues, and find a banal resolution at the end. So your romances are spoiled. When you are full of your own strong gusto of things, real old English strong gusto it is, like those tulips,[21] then I like you very much. But you shouldn't compare the sun to the yolk of an egg, except playfully. And you shouldn't spoil your story-poems with a sort of vulgar, artificial "flourish of ink." If you had followed the real tragedy of your man, or woman, it had been something.

I suppose you think me damned impertinent. But I hate to see you posturing, when there is thereby a real person betrayed in you.

Please don't be angry with what I say. Perhaps it really is impertinence.

At any rate, thank you very much for your book of poems, which I like because after all they have a lot of you in them — but how much nicer, finer, bigger you are, intrinsically, than your poetry is. Thank you also very much for the beautiful typewriter, with which both myself and my wife are for the present bewitched.

We are still staying on here — scarcely find it possible to move. It is cold, as you predict, but I think quite healthy. I am well, and Frieda is well. I am just finishing a book, supposed to be on Thomas Hardy, but in reality a sort of Confessions of my Heart. I wonder if ever it will come out[22] — & what you'd say to it.

I wonder if you saw Mitchell Kennerley. Pinker, the agent, is always worrying me about what he is to do with the American publishing of the novel Kennerley holds at present, in MS. Tell me if you saw him, will you.

We are not so sad any more: it was perhaps a mood, brought on by the war, and the English autumn. Now the days are brief but very beautiful: a big red sun rising and setting upon a pale, bluish, hoar-frost world. It is very beautiful. The robin comes on to the door-step now, and watches me as I write. Soon he will come indoors. Then it will be mid-winter.

I wish the war were over and gone. I will not give in to it. We who shall live after it are more important than those who fall.

Give our very warm regards to Mrs Russell.

Saluti di cuore

D. H. Lawrence

Tante belle cose from my wife to you and to Mrs Russell.

8

Nov. 27, 1914[23]

My dear Mr. Lawrence:

I have a lot to say, so much that I do not know where to begin. Your letters of October 16th are here and I trust you have received the typewriter safely. In fact I know you have, because I had a letter from the man who shipped it to you and he told me he had received a letter from you saying it had arrived. I trust it is working well and is really a convenience.

I have seen Mitchell Kennerley and he has refused all the poems I sent him for the "Forum" to pay me back for dunning him, but my dunning was of the mildest possible kind. I assumed that there had been some mistake about his paying you but I told him that mistake had prevented your going back to Italy, and that the money would be a very great convenience. I also told him that I did not think you looked very well, which I thought might move him a little. He denied that he owed you more than 10 pounds, 7 shillings and sixpence, but said he would send it the next day. I tried to get him to pay it to me and at first he said he would, but he wrote me a letter the next day saying that it would be less confusing if he sent it directly to you. I felt that quite probably he would never send it at all, but I could do nothing without your contract and list of the payments you have received. He was very much worried over your new book, afraid to print it as it stood. He said he should write you and suggest making certain changes. I, of course, could do nothing as it was none of my business and as I did not know [how] much you wish to break with him. Now I have seen Ferris Greenslet of Houghton Mifflin Company.[24] He is very enthusiastic over your books and said that he would consider publishing a volume of your short stories if you would send it along for him to see. Of course he cannot definitely decide without seeing them. I believe Houghton Mifflin and Company to be the most completely honest of any publishers over here. On the other hand I imagine that they are less daring in what they are willing to do in the matter of novelties than the Macmillan Company, but if you care to have them see your short stories with a view to publication send them along at once addressed to Ferris Greenslet, Esq. Houghton Mifflin Company, 4 Park Street, Boston Mass., and in your letter mention that these are the stories I spoke about to him.

Now as far as Mitchell Kennerley is concerned there is one way to get what you are due out of him and an absolutely sure way. If you will send me the contract and a list of what you have already received on account I will put it into the hands of some of my young lawyer friends who will promptly collect the money. This will cost you nothing as I tell you they are friends of mine. Ne[ith]er will my name appear as the lawyers will [   ] that this will make Kennerley see that he cannot treat you in the cavalier manner he has heretofore done. Of course there is no use attempting this unless you have all the legal documents to prove him in error. I sincerely hope that Mitchell Kennerley did send the money but the man impresses me as a very slippery customer and it would not surprise me at all to hear that he has not done it.

I wonder whether you have got my book yet. You have not mentioned it, but Richard Aldington writes that he has got his copy and I have also heard from another copy which I sent to England. I do hope your silence does not mean utter disapproval. It is discouraging work, writing, particularly if one insists upon writing as one wants and not as the publishers want. I am awfully down and out about it, but this down and outne[ss] is a chronic condition of us writers pe[rhaps].

The anthology is coming on with c[ontinu]al hitches, but I hope to get that fixe[ed up] in time. It is cold and bleak here out[   ]. Ada is in Salt Lake City because her father is dying, and I [am] alone with my seven dogs who, however, make excellent company. I wish so often that I could see you and Mrs. Lawrence. Please tell her that any of your manuscripts, prose or verse, would be most acceptable and I would consider myself honoured if she would send me some. This letter is to her too. I am not writing on separate pieces of paper because I am sure she is reading it over your shoulder now. Please excuse a typewritten letter. I am up to the eyes in work with my French lectures[25] and this is the quickest way. Do you think you will go back to Italy? If so do not forget to give me your address.

When I make a world I am going to eliminate distance, it is a very heart-rending thing. Please let me hear from you as soon as possible about the Kennerley thing and also what you think of my book. This silence fills my mind with evil apprehensions.

With very best wishes to you both,

9

The Triangle
Bellingdon Lane, *Chesham*, Bucks.
18 Dec 1914

My dear Amy Lowell,

The day before yesterday came your letter. You sound so sad in it. What had depressed you? — your book of poems, that they perhaps are stupid about in the papers? But there, they are always like that, the little critics. If the critics are not less than the authors they criticise, they will at once burst into equal authorship. And being less than the authors they criticise, they must diminish these authors. For no critic can admit anything bigger than himself. And we are all, therefore, no bigger than our little critics. So don't be sad. The work one has done with all ones might is as hard as a rock, no matter how much one suffers the silly slings & arrows in one's silly soft flesh.

Thank you very much indeed for going to Mitchell Kennerley for me. I hope you are not serious when you say that in so doing you have spoiled the "Forum" for yourself as a publishing field. Is Kennerley indeed such a swine? As for what he owes me — he does not send it, even if it is only ten pounds. I haven't kept proper accounts with him, because Duckworths made the agreement & all that. I will write to them. I also will write to Pinker, to see what he can do. I *must* get this novel out of Kennerley's hands, that he has in MS.

I am re-writing it. It will be called The Rainbow. When it is done, I think really it will be a fine piece of work.

My book of Short stories is out.[26] I am sending you a copy. I don't think it is doing very well. The critics really hate me. So they ought.

My wife and I we type away at my book on Thomas Hardy, which has turned out as a sort of Story of My Heart:[27] or a Confessio Fidei: which I must write again, still another time: and for which the critics will plainly beat me, as a Russian friend says.[28]

It is Christmas in a week today. I am afraid you may not get this letter in time: which is a pity. We shall be in this cottage. We shall have a little party at Christmas Eve. I at once begin to prick up my ears when I think of it. We shall have a great time, boiling ham and roasting chickens, and drinking chianti in memory of Italy. There will be eight of us, all nice people. We shall enjoy ourselves afterwards up in the attics. You wait. I shall spend 25/– on the spree, and do it quite rarely.

England is getting real thrills out of the war, at last. Yesterday & today there is the news of the shelling of Scarboro. I tell you the whole country is thrilled to the marrow, and enjoys it like hot punch.—I shall make punch at our Christmas Eve party, up in the attics with a Primus stove.

We have been in the midlands seeing my people, & Frieda seeing her husband.[29] He did it in the thorough music-hall fashion. It was a surprise visit. When we were children, and used to play at being grand, we put an old discarded hearthrug in the wheelbarrow, and my sister, perched there in state "at home," used to be 'Mrs Lawson' & I, visiting with a walking stick, was 'Mr Marchbanks.' We'd been laughing about it, my sister & I. So Frieda, in a burst of inspiration, announced herself to the landlady as 'Mrs Lawson.'

"You—" said the quondam husband, backing away—"I hoped never to see you again."

Frieda: "Yes—I know."

Quondam Husband: "And what are you doing in *this* town?"

Frieda: I came to see you about the children.

Quondam Husband: Aren't you ashamed to show your face where you are known? Isn't the commonest prostitute better than you?

Frieda: Oh no.

Quon. Husb.: Do you want to drive me off the face of the earth, Woman? Is there no place where I can have peace?

Frieda: You see I must speak to you about the children.

31

Quon Husb.: You shall *not* have them—they don't want to see you.

Then the conversation developed into a deeper tinge of slanging—part of which was:

Q. H.: *"If* you had to go away, why didn't you go away with a *gentleman?"*

Frieda: He is a *great* man.

Further slanging.

Q. Husb.: Don't you know you are the vilest creature on earth?

Frieda: Oh no.

A little more of such, & a departure of Frieda. She is no further to seeing her children.

Q. Husb: Don't you know, my solicitors have instructions to arrest you, if you attempt to interfere with the children.

Frieda: I don't care.

If this weren't too painful, dragging out for three years, as it does, it would be very funny, I think. The Quondam Husband is a Professor of French Literature, great admirer of Maupassant, has lived in Germany & Paris, & thinks he is the tip of cosmopolitan culture. But poor Frieda can't see her children.—I really give you the conversation verbatim.

It is very rainy & very dark. I shall try to get back to Italy at the end of January.

Give my sincere sympathy to Mrs Russell. I hope things aren't going *very* badly with her. All Christmas greetings to you.

D. H. Lawrence

I do wish we might have a Christmas party together. I feel like kicking everything to the devil and enjoying myself willy-nilly: a mild drunk and a great and rowdy spree.

[Frieda Lawrence begins writing]

It was rather mean of us to ask you to see Kennerley—But he is a pig—He gave Lawrence 25£ for "Sons & Lovers", promised him another 25£, then arrived the bad cheque—Dont bother anymore, only he must not have the new novel, but Pinker can see to that—L. hates the whole business so much that he shouts at me every time he thinks of it! I feel a grudge against Kennerley not only has he done me out of 25£, but every time L thinks of *Kennerley* he gets in a rage with *me,* the logic of men and husbands—You knew about

32

my nice children and what I have had to go through—I wish I could tell you all about, you are so bighearted, we think of you with great affection, one of the few oasis' in this desert world! We will go to Italy soon, as soon as we have a little money—I hope you received our letters, when you wrote you had not got our last—Our Italy address is: *Lerici* per Fiascherino
　　　　Golfo di Spezia

[Lawrence interjects] (but we're not gone yet)　[He also adds] I shall get some money in January all right. DHL

[Frieda continues] I wish you could come and see us soon!

　　　　　　　　　　Yours with many good wishes

　　　　　　　　　　Frieda L—

Poor Mrs Russel what a horrid time for her!

10

1, Byron Villas,
Vale-of-Health,
Hampstead,
London.
15 Sept 1915.

Dear Amy Lowell,

I wonder how you are and what you are doing. We have taken a flat here, and shall stay the winter through, I expect.

Thank you for the copy of the Imagiste.[30] It was a nice little volume, I thought. I don't know in the least how the English edition has done.

I am very busy with a lot of work—a novel coming out on the 30th of this month, a book of Italian & German studies soon.[31] Then we are doing this little paper.[32] It is the attempt to get at the real basis from which to start a reconstructive idea of this life of ours. I think you will be really interested. I wonder if you would care to subscribe, & to ask any serious people who care about the last questions of life to subscribe too.

At any rate, write & tell us how you are and what you are doing in America.

Yours very Sincerely

D. H. Lawrence

My wife sends greetings. I am always *very* grateful for the typewriter.

11

D. H. Lawrence,
1 Byron Villas,
Vale-of-Health,
Hampstead, London.

Forgive my delay in sending money. There is more to come in February. Send poems for new anthology soon as possible. Count on them. Letter follows this. Love to both.

Amy Lowell.

Cabled Dec. 15, 1915.
$4.20.

12

December 15, 1915.

My dear Mr. Lawrence:

I have so many apologies to make you that I hardly know where to begin. In the first place, my long silence. I am not a good correspondent, in fact I am a wretched one. The days and weeks go by without my realizing that I have not written. It has always been the curse of my existence, putting off letters, and what makes it particularly bad is that I have not yet sent you the money for your royalties. I was quite ill during the summer and struggling with the proofs of my new book,[33] and when I heard that you had moved,

I did not have your address; but I have had your address now for nearly two months.

I cabled you the money to-day, so that at least I know that you have got it safely, and I hope it will be all the more welcome coming as it does just before Christmas. I can only ask you to forgive me and assure you that it shall never happen again. I will send off your royalties, if I have any, without waiting to write a letter, which is the safest way. And by the way, there will be more royalties, and possibly larger ones, on the first of February, as Houghton Mifflin pay their authors twice a year. I am distributing the gross receipts, that is, I am not deducting for printing or advertising. That is my share towards helping the good work along.

We are planning the second Anthology now (you know, I signed an agreement with them for three years), and I am anxiously waiting for your contributions. All the others have sent theirs, but I have not received yours yet, and I must say I am not astonished considering my silence, but you must know by this time that that silence was one of the pen, not of the heart. I suppose hardly a week goes by that Mrs. Russell and I do not mention you and Mrs. Lawrence, and wish very much that we could see you.

I thank you a thousand times for sending me "The German Lieutenant."[34] The book is intensely interesting and vivid as it can be. I have not seen it issued over here. Has it been? I am deeply grieved by all this rumpus over "The Rainbow,"[35] and I am annoyed with myself that my silence prevented you from sending it to me, as I am extremely anxious to read it. Richard writes me that they are taking the matter up in Parliament, in which case I suppose you will really have more success in the end than if there had been no fuss. I think your publishers behaved abominably in abandoning you. They tell me that the book is to be issued over here, and now that Anthony Comstock[36] is dead, I do not suppose you have anything to fear. I have written Richard to procure me a copy by hook or by crook if he can, for you know you have no more fervent admirer in the world than I am. This wretched war which keeps us all apart is a terrible thing. I have thought so often of our two pleasant dinners together in my rooms at the Berkeley and of that delightful afternoon which you and Mrs. Lawrence gave us at Chesham. We did have good times. I hope we shall have some more, lots of them.

Richard writes me that you are going to Florida. Florida is not exactly Massachusetts, and I have never been there, and I am afraid the chances of our meeting, if you stay in Florida, are about the same as they would be if you stayed in London. Are you sailing direct to Florida, or are you going via New York? Because if the latter, I will make a special trip on there in order to go and pay you a little call.

Richard writes me that the Georgian Anthology[37] sold out its first edition in a day. That is magnificent. I congratulate you. It took us six months to attain a second edition, but there has been more written about us in the papers this last year than about anybody else except Masters and Verhaeren.[38] I do not know whether you have seen Masters' "Spoon River Anthology" so I am sending it to you, with the pleasantest greetings of the season. If you have already read it, pass it on to some one who has not. I think it a very great book, and I think you will agree with me.

I have been reading your poems round a good deal in a lecture I have been giving here and in New York and before various women's colleges; and I read several of your things the other day before the Poetry Society of America. Imagism is still considered a freak in London, I imagine, but in America it is already being taken seriously by a number of people, although others still jeer. The interest has been simply enormous, hardly a day passes that I do not receive a clipping of some kind, from somewhere, about it. I have been sending them all to Richard, so that you can easily get him to show them to you. Most of them, of course, are just silly, newspaper nonsense; but even the amount of them indicates a public interest, and there seems to be a general impression now that we are serious, hardworking artists, and not freaks.

I have just written a long book on "Six French Poets," but I did not send it to you because I thought that you would not care for it. I remember your wrestling with me last year was because of my French pose. You see it is not a pose, it is a reality, and if you do come to New York, you will see why it is a reality. You will realize that America now is more Continental than British. The immigration that has been going on for years is having an effect, and even we who are of pure Anglo-Saxon ancestry can not help being affected by it.

Please tell Mrs. Lawrence that I wish we could have a good talk together. She must be even madder at the fools who suppressed your book than you are. Here in America we should smile and say it is a good advertisement. And indeed, I think it can do you no harm in the end. It will be a big asset to the American sales; and if Parliament orders your book re-issued, as Richard seems to think

36

they will, I cannot imagine anything that would sell more like hot cakes.

By the way, I am enclosing five shillings. Will you see that two subscriptions to the "Signature" are sent to me? I meant to have sent it long ago. I trust the earlier numbers are not all out of print.

Now please, dear Mr. Lawrence, forgive me for my silence. Please both of you realize that it never means anything but just business and haste. I have been fearfully rushed and bothered this year with that French book. I pegged at it for eleven hours a day and nearly went under in the process. And remember, whether I am silent or not, my friendship never changes and my admiration never wavers.

Very sincerely and faithfully yours,

13

Porthcothan, St. Merryn, Padstow, Cornwall
20 Jan. 1916.

My dear Amy,

I have got my poetry MS. books from Italy, and hasten to send you some more verses, in case it is not too late for the anthology.[39] Perhaps you will like some of these. Tomorrow I will send more.

We are here in Cornwall till March: by the sea it is beautiful and wild. But I am ill in bed again. I have been ill a good deal this winter.

Dear Amy, will you hand on to Harriett Monroe the poems you do not want—or save them for me in America. I have got quite enough stuff now for a new book. Do you know who would best publish it in America? I shall need some money badly by the early summer, for there is nothing in prospect.

It is a pity you are so far off. Do write and tell me about yourself, and your poetry, and America.

If any of this poetry has been published in America, perhaps you will remember. But I don't think it has.

Many greetings from us both

D. H. Lawrence

14

My dear Amy,

I sent you some more poems, I should be so glad if they could arrive in time for the anthology. But will you at once *cancel* the last five stanzas from "Drunk", so that it ends with "Keep with you the troth I trowed". Do this for me hastily, Dear Amy, I hate those last five stanzas.

I find I have such a lot of poems, now, and such nice ones. I can make a most beautiful book.

I am still kept indoors by my inflammation but hope soon to be out.

I expect you to write to me *at once* remember, not to delay for a year. Mrs Aldington said how beautiful your poems for the anthology are — she is going to send them me. I do hope mine will come in time for the anthology, I begin to feel so keen about it.

Yours

D. H. Lawrence

15

February 1, 1916.

My dear Lawrence:

Your letter of January 10th was very welcome.[40] Of course, we shall remain friends. What on earth could prevent it? I am a bad correspondent, I know, but as I told you in my last letter, I am a loyal friend.

Your letter containing your poems came some time ago. I did not answer it because I did not have your address, and I hoped I should have your address soon, so I waited. The poems are excellent for our purpose. The one I like the best is "Erinyes," which I think is extraordinarily fine. "Resurrection" is not exactly the type I most care for personally, but that has not prevented me from recognizing it as interesting and very well done, and your crocus and cyclamen constantly coming in as a refrain, and as an ideal, is beautiful. But "Erinyes" gives me the greatest possible pleasure, and I think will have a very fine success.

I have sent Richard a copy of the Preface which Fletcher and I have written. It merely explains the things which the critics and the public seem unable to understand, and is mostly technical.[41] I know you are not so much interested in the technical side of verse as we are; indeed technique is only a means to an end, and the reason one talks about it is because other people do not seem to understand it. The fundamentals of poetry do not change, it is only the mode of expression that differs.

What you say about England I feel sure is true and intensely sad. I saw it coming years ago, long before the war. I am afraid it was one or two poems on the subject in "Sword Blades" which have prevented me from having any sort of recognition or sale in England. Let us hope, however, that something will come to deflect the issue, and that, as England has always succeeded in riding out every storm, she may still do so with that wonderful power of recuperation which seems to be inherent in the Anglo-Saxon blood.

I think you are right about the Aldingtons. I do think it is a poor kind of life. I wish they would come over here. I have urged them and begged them to do so. They hate America, I know, but really they do not know anything about it. Hilda was only a school-girl—a misunderstood and out of place school-girl—who mistook her own environment for the country at large, and Richard is merely prejudiced, and with no real grounds for the prejudice. He apparently gets his feeling about America from Ezra Pound and Hilda. But why should he not take it as well from Fletcher and me, both of whom he likes? America is young, it is crude, but it is sincere, and vital and open-minded. It has one quality which is both an advantage and a disadvantage—it is a disadvantage to smug satisfaction, but an advantage in exciting to effort—that is, that no success here will carry a man's poor work, if he makes a success with one book, he must keep writing good books to retain his position; he cannot live and sell on a past glory. The country is too honest and too little a respecter of persons to do as they do in England: find everything a man does good, simply because he has attained a certain position. I find it a stimulating place to live and work in and I think you will, too, and I think the Aldingtons would, if they could once make up their minds to come here, and take the country a little more broad-mindedly than they seem inclined to do at present.

I am awfully sorry that I have not been able to read your "Rainbow." I asked Richard to send it, as I wrote you, but I suppose he could not get a copy. It is not out here, apparently, as immediately on receipt of your letter saying that Huebsch was publishing it, I telephoned to the bookshop, only to be told that it was not yet announced for publication. As soon as it does come out, I shall get it and read it, and write you what I think of it, since you ask me to do so.

I suppose we shall have some more royalties in a day or two. They have not come in yet, but you may be sure I shall send them as soon as they do this time, and I will also send you copies of the Anthology, when it is out. Richard takes so long in answering letters that I do not know when we shall come out. We ought to be out in April, and if he would only hurry a little more, we could be. However, we shall come out sometime anyway.

Mrs. Russell joins me in kindest greetings to you both. Write again soon.

Very sincerely yours,

16

February 15, 1916.

Dear Lawrence:

Thank you very much for your nice letters and for the poems; and incidentally, here is a money-order for $36.51, being one-sixth of $219.08. This is gross receipts, not net, as I have no desire whatever to make any money out of the transaction, so I have not charged any of the expenses off against the contributors.

Fletcher and I went through your first batch of poems last week, and decided that some of these were more appropriate to our Anthology than "Resurrection," which you sent us in the beginning. We decided to take "Erinnyes," "At a Window," "Brooding Grief," "For Trouble and Shame," and "Perfidy" for the Anthology; and just now comes your new batch of poems.[42] I have not had time to read them yet, and there may be another here which we could add. Our original arrangement, you remember, was either seven short poems, or one long one and five short ones, or two long ones and three short ones, or three long ones. Now you have one long one and four short ones, so you are entitled to another short one. As there is not time to consult Richard and Hilda about this, we shall have to go it blind; but they have given us permission to do as we think best. The book is going to press the end of this week.

I took in the little lot of poems I had to Ferris Greenslet the other day, and left them with him, hoping that he would want them for one of the Autumn volumes of the New Poetry Series; but I am afraid the affair of "The Rainbow" has frightened him a little, and he does not dare take the risk. If you had the whole manuscript of the book ready and put together, and there were nothing in it to frighten him off (and he is not over prudish), I think he might accept it, but he did not feel inclined to do so from a fragment. He did tell me, however, that if you would take the book to Constable, he would authorize you to say from him that, if they publish it in England, Houghton Mifflin would order an edition of two hundred copies for America. I think this is probably as good an offer as you are likely to receive from the older and better-established publishers. It is possible that Knopf or Lawrence Gomme might consider the idea favourably. I will see Gomme when I go to New York next week, and sound him. Knopf I do not know, and I think there would be very little use offering him the book until we have a complete manuscript to show him. Mitchell Kennerly I do not advise, and I personally emphatically refuse to have anything to do with any transaction of which he is another party. Duffield might consider it; but I think in the case of many of these people who seem to be publishing works which are not likely to have a very great sale, they are usually given assistance by the author. Evidently there is some reason why you do not take the book to Huebsch; if he is publishing your "Rainbow," that would seem the natural thing to do. I really think if you can get Constable to consider it for England, with Houghton Mifflin's proposition to help them along, that would be as satisfactory a solution as any you can find.

I am awfully sorry that you are ill. I do hope the Spring will bring an improvement in your health. An English Winter is a very trying thing. You will, I am sure, be better when you pitch your tent in our warmer, sunnier climate.

This is not much of a letter, because I am too fearfully busy just now to write one. I am getting out the second edition of my book

41

on the French poets, trying to get together a volume of poems to be published in the Autumn,[43] and delivering two lectures next week in New York. These activities do not give me much leisure; but I have learned from bitter experience, as you know, that it is better to write at once than wait until I have time. And despite its shortness, this takes every short of kind remembrance and good wish to you both.

Very sincerely yours,

P.S. If you will send me your complete manuscript, I will try and see what I can do. But do try Constable at once!

17

The Tinners Arms—Zennor—St. Ives Cornwall.
1st March 1916

My dear Amy,

Thank you very much for your letter, & for all the thought you have taken for me. Constables here have refused my poems: so much the worse for them. Pinker says he will try *Doran* in America. I don't think Pinker is very good at America: and I do put my hopes in your country. We must see what we can do.

Thank you very much also for the money. You are most generous.

I will let you know how things develop with my poems. All good luck to your new volume; & your lectures.

With regards from my wife & me.

Yours

D. H. Lawrence

18

My dear Amy,

I got the two copies of the new Imagiste on Saturday. It looks very nice, as usual, the book. And I think it is *quite* up to the mark, don't you? It should make a considerable impression. Tell me what the reviewers say, if you have time, will you?

Will Constable publish the book in England? If so I can get another copy or two. If not I must write to America for a couple.

My "Twilight in Italy" and a book of poems "Amores" are both to be published in New York by Doran: at least, I have signed the agreement.[44] I will send you the "Twilight in Italy" when it comes: it is due any day now, here.

For news, we have always the same: we are gaily ringing our last shilling, for the empty heavens to hear it. We have got a very lovely little cottage *of our own* here, rent £5– a year, looking down on the sea. There are sea-pinks, like little throngs of pink bees hovering on the edge of the land, over a sea that is blue and hard like a jewel. There are myriad primroses spread out so large and cool and riskily, under the shadows, and bluebells trailing under the great granite boulders, and fox-gloves rearing up to look. It is rather a wild, rocky country, of magpies and hawks and foxes. I love it.

The "Compulsion" comes into force June 24th. I suppose they will leave me alone, because of my health. If only the war would end! It is so bitterly meaningless now.

Have you any news? It is time now that the miracle should happen—the Lord suddenly shouting out of the thunder "Fous-moi la paix, là-bas,"[45] like a man just waked up.

Many greetings from my wife & me.

Yours

D. H. Lawrence

19

Dear Lawrence:

I am enclosing a draft for £8–1–7, which represents the royalties on "Some Imagist Poets" 1915 and 1916, up to the first of August. The sale of the new volume is within 35 copies of the sale of the 1915 volume at this same date, which shows an extraordinary sustaining of interest in our work, I think. Houghton Mifflin behaved very badly in regard to the English edition. By some lapse in the office arrangements, they did not keep after Constable and see that they took a certain number of copies, and C. sidestepped, either on purpose or from inadvertence, so that I discovered, about three weeks ago, that no copies had been sent to England. Of course, I was extremely angry and made an awful fuss, and they apologized most humbly and said that their contract with Constable was such that they would be obliged to take the book, and that they would see to it at once. But of course no English sales appear in this statement, which is as follows:

249	Imagist Poets,	1915.	.36¼	$90.26
389	"	"	1916.	.36¼	141.01
				231.27

The new book is not making as much clamour as the first one did because people no longer consider us as freaks, but are taking us seriously. The clamour had its effect as advertising, but the much more serious and lengthy reviews we are now receiving are a pleasant tribute. I am sending you a copy of the June-July "Little Review" which contains the very nice criticism of our work by Mrs. Aldis. I trust you will like my poem in the same number. Also "The Poetry Review" has a short notice by Professor Phelps of Yale[46] about us, which I am also sending.

I am looking forward with great interest to your two new volumes, "Italian Sketches" and "Poems." I trust you will send them to me.

I am glad to know that you are in St. Ives for, although I have never been there, I believe it to be a beautiful place, and your description of the cowslips and other things is charming, but then I do not know anybody that writes about the English countryside as you do; I had rather read what you say about it than look at it, which is a high tribute.

Mrs. Russell and I have come up here for the Summer,[47] as I always do when I am not in Europe. You would like this place, it is all hills, and rushing brooks, and clear, placid lakes.

The war looks to me as if it were about over. I certainly hope so. I am homesick for you all and want to go back to England, which I love so much.

Harriett Monroe, in this month's "Poetry" says awfully nice things about your "Erinnyes."[48] I am sending you that, too.

With kind rembrances to Mrs. Lawrence and yourself from Mrs. Russell and me,

Always affectionately yours,

20

Higher Tregerthen, Zennor, St. Ives
Cornwall
23 August 1916

My dear Amy

Thank you so much for the cheque for £8, which came today. Those Imagiste books seem to blossom into gold like a monthly rose. I am very glad, too, to hear of the good things the papers are deigning to say. You should see my English critics walking round me in every sort of trepidation, like dogs round a mongoose.

I will ask Duckworths to send you the poems & the Italian Sketches.[49] You know we may only send books abroad, through the publisher or a bookseller. Otherwise, of course, I should gladly autograph them for you.

Thank God they did not make me a soldier. I had to join up, & spent a night in barracks, and then they gave me a total exemption. If they hadn't, I should have been a stretched corpse in a fortnight: that I knew, at four o clock in the morning, on that fatal night in barracks at Bodmin. There is something in military life that would kill me off, as if I were in an asphyxiating chamber. The whole thing is abhorrent to me—even the camaraderie, that is so glamorous—the Achilles & Patroclus business. The spirit, the pure spirit of militarism is sheer death to a nature that is at all constructive or social-creative. And it is not that I am afraid or shy: I can get on with the men like a house on fire. It is simply that the spirit of militarism is essentially destructive, destroying the individual and the constructive social being. It is *bad*. How Aldington will stand it I don't know. But I can tell that the glamour is getting hold of him: the "now we're all men together" business, the kind of love that was between Achilles & Patroclus. And if once that lays hold of a man, then farewell to that man forever, as an independent or constructive soul.

I am glad you think the war is virtually over. Official London seems to be saying, with much confidence, two more years of it. But nobody knows. God help us if this is going on for two years more. These last two years have made one at least two centuries older. In two years more, we shall have ceased to be human beings at all. Certainly England has spit on her hands and taken hold at last. The whole nation is hanging on tense and taut, throwing all her weight on the rope at last, in the tug of war. It is our tradition—to get our blood up at the eleventh hour. Well, the English blood is up now, the bull-dog is hanging on—alas that it ever need have come to pass. What will be the end, when the war *is* at last over, the mind refuses to consider: but it will be nothing good.

So one's soul knows misfortune and terror. But there is a limit to grief for one's fellow man: one becomes callous, since nothing can be done.

Here we live very quietly indeed, being far from the world. Here we live as if on one of the blessed Isles, the moors are so still behind us, the sea so big in front. I am very much better, much stronger, now. All the winter I was so ill. I hope it won't be so again this year. But I think not. I am busy typing out a new novel, to be called "Women in Love." Every day I bless you for the gift of the typewriter. It runs so glibly, & has at last become a true confrère. I take so unkindly to any sort of machinery. But now I & the type writer have sworn a Blutbruderschaft.[50]

We go down & bathe among the rocks—not the typewriter, but Frieda & I. Today there were great rollers coming from the west. It is so frightening, when one is naked among the rocks, to see the high water rising to a threatening wall, the pale green fire shooting along, then bursting into a furious wild incandescence of foam. But it is great fun. It is so lovely to recognise the non-human elements: to hear the rain like a song, to feel the wind going by one, to be thrown against the rocks by the wonderful water.

I cannot bear to see or to know humanity any more.

Your remoter America must be splendid. One day, I hope to come to see it, when there is peace and I am not poor. We are living on credit as usual. But what does it matter, in a world like this. Hilda Aldington says to me, why don't I write hymns to fire, why am I not in love with a tree. But my fire is a pyre, & the tree is the tree of Knowledge.

I wonder if I have said anything censurous in my letter—I think not. The honeysuckle smells so sweet tonight—what are the flowers in New Hampshire? Often I have longed to go to a country which has new, quite unknown flowers & birds. It would be such a joy to make their acquaintance. Have you still got humming birds, as in Crèvecoeur? I liked Crèvecoeur "Letters of an American Farmer," *so* much. And how splendid Hermann Melvilles "Moby Dick" is, & Dana's "Two Years before the Mast." But your classic American Literature[51] I find to my surprise, is *older* than our English. The tree did not become new, which was transplanted. It only ran more swiftly into age, impersonal, non-human almost. But how good these books are! Is the *English* tree in America almost dead? By the literature, I think it is.

Remember me warmly to Mrs Russell. Many greetings to you from my wife & me. You will never come back to the England you knew before. But at any rate, when you do come, you must come here.

D. H. Lawrence

Doran is to publish both the books of mine in America.

21

**Higher Tregerthen, Zennor, St. Ives.
Cornwall.
12 Oct. 1916**

My dear Amy,

I don't know whether you would get my last letter, which I sent to the New Hampshire address, and also the two books of mine, which Duckworths told me they forwarded to you. I hope they reach you safely, and will give you a little pleasure. You must tell me how you like them.

Hilda Aldington asked me for some things for the new anthology. I sent several pieces of verse along: don't know what she will think of them. They are mostly very regular. I must see if Harriett Monroe will publish something of mine.

I am still typing away at my new novel: it takes a tremendous time: and the novel itself is one of the labours of Hercules. I shall be glad when it is done. Then I must really set to and write short stories such as the magazines may be prevailed upon to publish. Alas, I am afraid I was not born to popularity.

The winter seems already to have come. The heather on the hills is dead, the bracken is dry and brown, and blowing away to nothingness. Already the fowls stand bunched-up motionless and disconsolate under the stacks, out of the wind, the sky is all grey and moving. One feels like a fowl oneself, hulking under the lee of the past, to escape the destructive wind of the present. The atmosphere all over the country is black and painful to breathe, one dare hardly move. Heaven send us happier days.

All good greetings from my wife & me.

D. H. Lawrence

22

Higher Tregerthen, Zennor, St. Ives, Cornwall.
14 Novem. 1916

My dear Amy

I was infinitely touched when there came this morning a cheque for £60, sent by you through the bankers. One is so moved by the kindness: the money, after all, is necessity, but the kindness is given. This I shall always treasure up, the kindness, even if I can pay you back the money. Because after all, there is not much real generosity in the world.

I was rather sorry Frieda wrote and asked you for money:[52] how do we know what you have to do with your money. But it is wearying, to be so much unwell, and penniless. I shall begin at once to move towards Italy: though heaven knows when we shall really get away. And I hope, from Italy, to come on to America, next year, when I am better and the winter has gone.

Why don't you come to Rome for a while? Think how jolly that would be, if we were all in Rome at the same time. Perhaps you would like it better, in these times, than London.

Your book, Men Women and Ghosts, came two days ago. We have both read all the poems. I like this book better than "Sword Blades." I think The Cremona Violin is both a lovely story and lovely verse: an exquisite picture into the bargain. Then I like The Fruit Shop, the sense of youngness and all the gorgeous fruitfulness in store, then the sudden destructiveness of Bonaparte, a smash of irony. I like that. Some of the movements of the Hammers really startle one's heart—one listens, and hears, and lives, it is almost frightening. Only I don't care for the Ship. "Reaping" seems to me one of the very best—a real straight jet of a story—but of course there isn't the newness of sensation one gets in Hoops—it belongs to the old knowledge—but it is *very* good. I always like "Spring Day"—sometimes the prose is best of all, better than any verse-form.—And then after all, I like Towns in Colour more than anything in the book: and of these Opera and Aquarium most.[53]

It is very surprising to me, now I have come to understand you Americans a little, to realise how much older you are than us, how much further you and your art are really, developed, outstripping us by far in decadence and non-emotional aestheticism, how much beyond us you are in the last stages of human apprehension of the physico-sensational world, apprehension of things non-human, not conceptual. We still see with concepts. But you, in the last stages of return, have gone beyond tragedy and emotion, even beyond irony, and have come to the pure mechanical stage of physical apprehension, the *human* unit almost lost, the primary elemental forces, kinetic, dynamic—prismatic, tonic, the great, massive, active, *inorganic* world, elemental, never softened by life, that hard universe of Matter and Force where life is not yet known, come to pass again. It is strange and wonderful. I find it only in you & H.D., in English: in your "Bath," and the fire of the lacquer music-stand, & Acquarium, & some Stravinsky, and here & there in Roxbury Garden—which, to my mind, is not quite chemical and crystollographical *enough.*[54] Of course, it seems to me this is a real *cul de sac* of art. You can't get any further than

> "Streaks of green & yellow iridescence
> Silver shiftings
> Rings veering out of rings
> Silver—gold—
> Grey-green opaqueness sliding down"

You see it is uttering pure sensation *without concepts*, which is what this futuristic art tries to do. One step further and it passes into *mere noises*, as the Italian futurismo poems have done, or mere jags and zig-zags, as the futuristic paintings. Then it ceases to be art, and is pure accident, mindless. — But there is this to fulfil, this last and most primary state of our being, where we are shocked into form like crystals that take place from the fluid chaos. And it is this primary state of being which you carry into art, in

> "Gold clusters
> Flash in soft explosions
> On the blue darkness
> Suck back to a point
> And disappear . . ."[55]

— for example. You might have called your book "Rockets and Sighs." It would have been better than Men Women & Ghosts.

If ever I come to America I will write about these things. But won't you try to come to Rome. Think of the Naples aquarium, and the Naples museum — and Rome itself. We might enjoy it so much.

Thank you once more, dear Amy. Remember me to Mrs Russell. My wife is writing to you. — I have just finished a novel, of which I am proud. — Did you get my "Amores" and "Twilight in Italy?" Do let us have a letter.

Yours ever

D. H. Lawrence

These things are your best, by far, I think: Spring day, Towns in Colour, Hammers, p. 344, some p. 346, & p. 347 of the Stravinsky. The shock and clipping of the physico-mechanical world are your finest expression.[56]
Do write a book called Fire Rockets.

23

Higher Tregerthen—Zennor, St. Ives, Cornwall
7 Dec. 1916

My dear Amy

We were very sorry to hear, from Mrs Russell's letters, that you were so ill. It must have been lacerating, and just at the time of your brother's death![57] I do hope you are better. I shall be glad to hear from you yourself, when you are well.

I am reviving quite a lot—even going out for walks again, and looking at the world. I think of going to London for a few days soon, to see everybody, for I have not left Cornwall for a whole twelve months. Heaven knows, the outer world does not look very inviting to me. But I must see people, and hear what they have to say.

There have been so many restrictions put on travelling, I don't know even now whether they will let us go to Italy—most probably not. I was disappointed—but there, one must be thankful if one can live in any kind of freedom at all, nowadays. I am thankful to be better in health, to be walking about and facing life again, so I won't grumble.

We have got Lloyd George for Prime Minister. That is a bad look-out for England. There was in Asquith the old English *decency*, and the lingering love of liberty. But Lloyd George is a clever little Welsh *rat*, absolutely dead at the core, sterile, barren, mechanical, capable only of rapid and acute mechanical movements. God alone knows where he will land us: there will be a very big mess. But the country at-large wanted him. "Quem Deus vult perdere—" All the time, when I look at my countrymen, my mind exclaims in amazement 'Whom the Gods wish to destroy, they first make mad.'[58]

I was glad to hear that your book was going so well: that will cheer you up. Yesterday I saw it advertised in the Times, but have not seen any reviews. I hope it will do well in England too.

We both wish you a peaceful and happy Christmas. Kindest greetings to Mrs Russell.

D. H. Lawrence

24

February 16, 1917.

My dear Lawrence:

I have so many things to thank you for that I do not know where to begin. I have enjoyed your "Twilight in Italy" immensely, and your "Amores" introduced some old friends and some new. I will write you a letter in detail about them very soon, but I have had the devil's own winter—two months in bed threatened with gall-stones and terribly ill, then a month in New York lecturing, and now, after a couple of weeks at home trying to pick up loose ends, I am off for the West on another lecturing tour of a month. I think these lecture tours help us all, but sometimes they do seem to take a good deal of time.

I am enclosing the statement of our account with Houghton-Mifflin up to the 1st of February. The $1.50 refers to a copy which was bound up especially for a subscriber and which they charged me for on the last bill by accident. Your share, or one-sixth of this amount of $167.65, is £5.–16,–2, for which I am enclosing draft.

You will be glad to hear that our first volume is in its third edition, our second volume in its second and that I am correcting the proofs of the third volume today. What may amuse you is that England sent for more copies of our first volume not longer ago than last month, showing that it is still selling there.

Your letter about my work gave me great pleasure, and your analysis of it was most interesting. I am sure you will be glad to know that the volume is already in its third edition, so that I really think that we may all regard ourselves as pretty successful. That hardly applies to you, however, as you have always been successful. You were the only one of us who had a reputation to start with. And great though it is, I hardly think it can be great enough, so much do I admire your work. It was the greatest possible pleasure to me to be able to help you the other day, and I hope that when you find yourself stuck again, you will not hesitate to apply to me.

Give my love to your wife and excuse the shortness and abruptness of this letter, but I really am so pressed for time I do not know what to do.

Very sincerely yours,

2 enclosures.

52

25

Higher Tregerthen, Zennor, St. Ives.
Cornwall
23 March 1917

My dear Amy

I received the other day your letter with cheque for £5, for the anthology, and was *very* glad to hear of you better in health, and busy.

Hilda Aldington sent me your Japanese poems, for the new anthology. I don't like them *nearly* so well as your other things, and I do wish you hadn't put them in. *Don't* do Japanese things, Amy, if you love us. I would a million times rather have a fragment of "Aquarium" than all the Japanese poems put together. I am so disappointed with this batch you have decided to put in, it isn't you at *all*, it has nothing to do with you, and it is not real. Alas and alas, why have you done this thing?

Hilda Aldington seems very sad and suppressed, everything is wrong. I *wish* things would get better. I have done a set of little essays called "The Reality of Peace", very important to me. I wish they would come out in America. They may appear in the English Review,[59] in which case I shall send them to you. Oh dear, it is a real struggle to get any further, we seem really stuck in a bog of wrongness. I wish above all things the tide would turn in the hearts of people, and make for creation & happiness: for we are almost lost. But we will hope on, & struggle.

Do write from your *real* Self, Amy, don't make up things from the outside, it is so saddening.

With love from both

D. H. Lawrence

26

My dear Lawrence: —

Here are your royalties for this half-year ending July 30th. The account is as follows: —

SALES

86 Imagist Poets, 1915 at	.36¼	31.17
226 " " , 1916 "	.36¼	81.92
50 " " , " to England		15.94
434 " " , 1917 at	.36¼	157.32
				286.35

286.35 divided by 6 — 47.72 — 9.16.4

I have enjoyed seeing your stories from time to time in "The Seven Arts."[60] That is the most interesting and alive paper over here to-day, and I am very glad you are one of the contributors. I am sorry you did not like my "Lacquer Prints" in the "Anthology," but really they are not artificial, as you seem to think. That is a perfectly authentic side of my nature. I never in my life wrote anything that was not sincere, and personally I like these little poems about as well as anything I have done.

If you see "The Seven Arts" you will see a long poem of mine in the August number,[61] but I am afraid you will not like this either. The tragedies and agonies of states are not so appealing as those of persons, as I am well aware, still the poem has made some friends.

I wish you would write and tell me how you and your wife are getting on. Give her my love and the same to you.

Sincerely yours,

27

My dear Amy

How are you, and what are you doing? It is ages since I have heard of or from you. How is your health, and what are you writing?

I am all right in health. Frieda has been laid low with neuritis in her leg: very bad for a month, but righting now. I think she'll soon be sound.

Here the community seriously thinks of building an ark, for the cataclysmic deluge has certainly set in. It rains and rains, and it blows the sea up on to the land, in volleys and masses of wind. We are all being finely and subtly sea-pickled, sea-changed, sure enough, "into something new and strange."[62] I shouldn't be a bit surprised to find one morning that fine webs had grown between my toes, and that my legs were slippery with sea-weedy Scales. I feel quite spray-blind, like any fish, and my brain is turning nacreous. I verily believe I am metamorphosed—feel as if I daren't look to see.

The corn is cut, and being washed back again to the bowels of the earth. I made a wonderful garden: but the pea-rows are already beaten and smashed and dissolved to nauseous glue, and the leaves are blown to bits from off the marrow vines, leaving the voluptuous smooth-skinned marrows naked like Virgins in the hands of the heathen. All's wrong with the world, in contradiction to Browning. But I don't care—why should I!

Nobody will publish my novel "Women in Love"—my best bit of work. The publishers say "it is too strong for an English public." Poor darling English public, when will it go in for a little spiritual athletics. Are these Tommies, so tough and brown on the outside, are they really so pappy and unbaked inside, that they would faint and fall under a mere dose of "Women in Love"?—Let me mix my metaphors thoroughly, let me put gravy-salt into the pudding, and pour vanilla essence over the beef, for the world is mad, yet won't cry "Willlow, Willow," and drown itself like Ophelia.

Chatto & Windus are this autumn bringing out a new book of verse of mine "Look, We Have Come Through." They are actually going to give me 20 guineas in advance of royalties.—I will send you a copy as soon as I can (not of the guineas).—This is a one bright beam in my publishing sky.—But I shall have to go and look for daylight with a lantern.

That is to say, with an eye to material things as well as spiritual: at last I am learning to squint:—I am doing a set of essays on "The Transcendental Element in American (Classic) Literature." It sounds very fine and large, but in reality is rather a thrilling blood-and-thunder, your-money-or-your-life kind of thing: hands-up, America!—No, but they are very keen essays in criticism—cut your fingers if you don't handle them carefully.—Are you going to help me to hold up the "Yale Review" or the "New Republic" or some such old fat coach, with this ten-barrelled pistol of essays of mine, held right in the eye of America? Answer me that, Donna Americana. Will you try to suborn for me the conductor of one of these coaches?—Never say nay.—Tis a chef-d'oeuvre of soul-searching criticism.—Shall I inscribe it to you? Say the word!

To
Amy Lowell
Who buttered my bread
These few fair words.
For she can butter her own parsnips.
Being well-to-do
She gave to the thankless
Because she thought it was worth it.

Frieda says you will be offended. Jamais de la vie![63] cry I.—But please yourself.

Ah me—it's a long way to Tipperary, if Tipperrary means a place of peacefulness.—I shall come to America directly the war is over. No doubt you don't want me—but it will be one of the moments of my life when I can say "Farewell and Adieu" to Europe; the "It is finished" of my Golgotha. As for Uncle Sam, I put my fingers to my nose, at him.

D. H. Lawrence

28

D. H. Lawrence
Higher Tregerthen, Sennor,
St. Ives, Cornwall
England.
November 13, 1917.

My dear Lawrence:

Your letter of the 30th of August is here, but I have not heard from you yet as to whether you received the royalty cheque I sent you some time ago. I hope you did; the others seem to have.

I sent you my new book, "Tendencies in Modern American Poetry," a few days ago. I hope you will find something in it you will like, but I do not think you will agree with much of it. However, that does not matter.

I am awfully sorry to hear that Mrs. Lawrence has had neuritis. That is a perfectly nasty thing. My brother-in-law had it once and I have never forgotten how much he suffered.

I am sorry to have to tell you what you probably know already, that "The Seven Arts" have discontinued publication. Some pacifist articles which they printed incensed the person who was backing them, a Mrs. Rankin, and she promptly withdrew her support, and they failed to raise the money to continue at this time, although they have a promise of a backer after the war is over. Their having gone under is a calamity to all of us of the younger school. There is no other magazine to take its place, and I do not know what we shall do now the conservatives have it all their own way.

I shall be very glad indeed to have you come to America when the war is over, and I do hope there is a chance of that time coming before we are all dead. I confess that occasionally it seems as though it were quite impossible that we should ever again live in a time of peace. It comes particularly hard on us artists for the uproar and agitation of war is not conducive to writing, and if it goes on long I am afraid it will put literature back irrevocably or rather for fifty years or more.

I wish there were anything I could do about helping you place your things, but now that the more radical magazines have disappeared from the field, it is hard for any of us of the newer tendencies to get accepted by conservative editors. Your name, however, is so well known that I should think it alone would carry. The only one of the older magazines which I think is likely to pay much attention to anything I say is "The North American Review." For some unknown reason they like my poetry, but they are very conservative indeed, and everything would have to be toned down for them, or carefully selected. I consider "The Yale Review," which you suggest, as one of the worst of the bunch, only beaten by "The Atlantic." In fact, for serious things like essay-writing or poetry, there is hardly any paper now that is sympathetic to the new work. I think "The New Republic" is the most hopeful, and I feel sure that if you were to write to them yourself you would stand a good deal of chance of being accepted, and I would certainly speak to the editors were I not sure it would do you more harm than good. They have just published a rather sniffy review of my new book. They gave it a prominent place, and then proceeded to air their own smartness and call it a review. I have found them most unsatisfactory to deal with and have practically ceased to be a contributor in consequence. For stories, of course, there are the illustrated magazines like "The Century," and "Scribners' ". I think "The Century" is the more open-minded of those two. "Harpers" is out of the question. "The Smart Set" you undoubtedly know. It is a cheap and clap-trap magazine, but is more willing to listen to things with a difference. It does not pay very well. Apart from these I can think of no magazines at present which care for anything but old-fashioned stuff. Of course the radical magazines had a less firm financial foundation than the more conservative ones, and I suppose that is the reason so many of them have ceased publication. "The Seven Arts," "Others," "The Masses," and "The Poetry Review" have all gone under. And "The Little Review," besides not paying anything, seems to have sold its soul bodily to Ezra Pound, and is not to me an agreeable place in which to publish any more.

Do write and tell me how you are getting on, and how Mrs. Lawrence is.

With best wishes for you both in which Mrs. Russell joins,

Always sincerely yours,

29

My dear Amy,

Your letter reached me yesterday: your book came a little earlier. This latter I had not acknowledged. But I had thanked you for the cheque for the Anthology, which I received some weeks back. — My publishers have sent you my new book of poems. I hope you will get it all right.

Since writing my last letter, everything has gone wrong with us. The police & military came and searched our house and turned us out of Cornwall — for no reason under the sun, except of course that Frieda is German by birth, and I am not warlike. So here we are cast upon a rather disagreeable world. Hilda like an angel came to the rescue and lent us her room. But now she and Richard are come back, we must yield it up & go down to the country to a cottage that can be lent us by another friend. When one has no money to pay for lodgings, it is no joke to be kicked out of one's house and home at random, & given nowhere to go. However, we shall get over it all.

My book "Look, we have Come Through" is out about a fortnight: as usual the critics fall on me: the Times says "the Muse can only turn away her face in pained distaste."[64] Poor Muse, I feel as if I had affronted a white-haired old spinster with weak eyes. But I don't really care what critics say, so long as I myself could personally be left in peace. This, it seems, cannot be. People write letters of accusation, because one has a beard and looks not quite the usual thing: and then one has detectives at one's heels like stray dogs, not to be got rid of. It is very hateful and humiliating and degrading. It makes me mad in my blood: so stupid and unnecessary. I want to be in quiet retreat in my own place in Cornwall — but they haul me out and then follow me round: really, [it] is too maddening. One would think they did it to amuse themselves.

I met Fletcher for the first time the other day. It surprised me to find him so nervously hyper-sensitive and fretted. I thought he was a rather hearty American type, from his poems. I was mistaken. But I liked him.[65]

The Aldingtons are in London — Richard has another fortnight or so: and then heaven knows where he will be sent: let us hope, somewhere in England. They seem pretty happy, as far as it is possible under the circumstances. We have had some good hours with them in Mecklenburgh Square—really jolly, notwithstanding everything: remembering that evening at the Berkeley with you, when we all met for the first time, and laughing at ourselves. Oh my dear Amy, I do wish to heaven we could all meet again in peace and freedom, to laugh together and be decent and happy with each other. This is a more wintry winter of discontent than I had ever conceived.—Never mind, the devil won't rampage in triumph for ever.

Frieda sends her love. We both hope that nice things will happen to you for Christmas: and we look forward to a meeting again—soon.

D. H. Lawrence

30

D. H. Lawrence, Esq.
c/o Mrs. Richard Aldington,
44 Mechlenburgh Square,
London, W. C. England.
12 March, 1918.

Dear Lawrence:

I have just sent a money order to Hilda for you. She told me that your address was uncertain as you were moving, and that I had better send everything direct to her. This money order represents royalties for our Imagist Anthologies of $12.74, plus a small donation of $200.00, which may come in handy. Here is the account:

SALES

26 Imagist Poets, 1915 at .36¼	$ 9.43
43 Imagist Poets, 1916 at .36¼	15.59
142 Imagist Poets, 1917 at .36¼	<u>51.47</u>
	$ 76.49

$76.49 divided by 6 — $12.74 — 2.14.0

Your new volume of poems has come and looks very interesting. I have been so crowded with work that I have not been able to really read it yet, but I am just starting on a review of all your work for one of my lectures. You are a bad fellow, and I am very much annoyed with you! Do you remember that I asked you weeks ago to send me an account of your life to be included in this lecture, and no such account have I ever received. This is too bad, as it would have been very interesting to my audience and also it rounds out my series of Imagist Poets, for this lecture is on the English Imagists;[66] you, and Richard and Flint, and I wanted to deal with you three as adequately as I did with Hilda and Fletcher in my book. I expect to publish these lectures later in a volume of essays, so I would be awfully glad if you would send me that biography as soon as possible anyway. I will send you a copy of my lecture when I get it written, that is, of the part referring to you, and then you will know exactly what I think of your book. Certainly you have had no more fervent or continued admirer of your work than I.

This is not much of a letter, because I never seem to have time for anything any more. The real letter that I should have written has gone into the essay.

Please give a great deal of love to your wife, and believe me always

Your sincere and affectionate friend,

31

Mountain Cottage
Middleton by Wirksworth
Derby. — England
18 June 1918

My dear Amy

I have just read your lectures — the one on me — which I got from Hilda. Thanks for the nice things you say about me. I don't mind what people think of my work, so long as their attitude is *passionately* honest — which I believe yours is. As for intellectual honesty, I care nothing for it, for it may rest on the most utterly false *a priori*.

I never thanked you for the dollars, either: not because I was not

61

grateful, but because sometimes one's soul is a dumb rock, and won't be either coaxed or struck into utterance. We were very glad of the help—it is always a case of touch and go, with us, financially.

I have just heard also that Huebsch is bringing out an edition of "Look We Have Come Through", in New York. I am glad of that. Perhaps America will like it better than England does. Nothing but shams go down here, just now. I suppose it is inevitable.

I have not seen Hilda for some time—but believe she is happy in Cornwall—as far as it is possible to be happy, with the world as it is.

I have just gathered a new MS. of a book of poems—"Coming Awake"—so named after the first poem.[67] I have worked at some of them for a long time—many years—but many are new, made this spring. I have just inscribed the MS. to you: simply put "to Amy Lowell." You must let me know if you would like this to stand. I finished the book, and made its list of contents, this very day—and I shall send it off today to Pinker. It is all different kinds of poems—nothing for anybody to take exception to, I believe. I hope you will like it.

We are here in Derbyshire, just near my native place—come home, in these last wretched days—not to die, I hope. Life is very wretched, really, in the outer world—and in the immediate world too, such a ghastly stress, a horrid pressure on one, all the time—and gnawing anxiety. The future seems utterly impenetrable, and as fathomless as the Bottomless Pit, and about as desperate.—But no doubt the world will sail out again, out of the Maelström. Perhaps even now it is moving clear from the Vortex.

I still want to come to America, to see you and the New World, when everything quiets down.

Frieda sends her love. Just let me know about the inscription.

Yours very Sincerely

D. H. Lawrence

32

D. H. LAWRENCE, ESQ
Mountain Cottage
Middleton by Wirksworth
Derby England.
22 July, 1918.

My dear Lawrence:

Of course I shall be delighted, more than delighted, really very much touched, to have you dedicate your manuscript to me. My admiration for your work is very great, as I think you must have seen in that all-too-brief notice at the end of the article which Hilda sent you.

I have not read anything for years which struck me as so powerful, so full of both reality and honesty as your "Look! We Have Come Through." I wish I could have written more about your work as I think it is all excellent, but of course, in that lecture, I was only speaking of poetry, and therefore tales and essays had no place. Some time I shall write an article devoted to you alone. Some day! Ah, that some day in which I am going to have time to carry out all my schemes. Frieda's account of your life, short as it was, did not reach me in time for the lecture, so I could not give anything of your biography.[68]

I am very glad to know that Huebsch is bringing out "Look! We Have Come Through," but I am sorry to know that it has not done well in England. May I tell you that I think that Futurist cover was too flippant an introduction to so serious a book as this? Perhaps the designer did not intend it to be flippant, but it is certainly too geometrical, what Ezra Pound describes as "Non-representative Art," to connote human emotion. It constantly announces its sincerity, but methinks "protests too much." I think it springs from jealousy for why—poetry and music have both grown in recent years. They have developed in a hundred ways, but for some reason painting has not kept pace with them. Possibly there are not as great painters alive to-day as there are poets and musicians, but naturally the painters have not wanted to admit this. Therefore they have sought an originality which, as it was not the result of natural growth, is at best freaky and factitious. In this case, the cover jars with the contents of your book as though it were a sneer set in front of a sacrament.

I will send you my new book which will be out in the Autumn.[69]
I have a feeling that you will not like it, but still I shall hope. Send
me your new volume when it comes out.

Mrs. Russell joins me with the kindest messages to both of you.

Very sincerely yours,

33

D. H. Lawrence, Esq.,
Mountain Cottage
Middleton By Wicksworth
Derby
England.
13 August, 1918.

Dear Lawrence:

It is only a minute ago since I wrote to you, but here are our
half-yearly royalties, not so large as I could wish, but of course you
know what the war has done for books.

SALES.

34 Imagist Poets,	1915.	at	.36¼	12.33
24 " "	1916.	"	.36¼	8.70
71 " "	1917.	"—	.36¼	25.74
				46.77

$46.77 divided by 6 — $7.79 or 1.11.9

As I wrote you last year, I am now letting the Anthologies go
out of print, as it seems to me their work has been accomplished.
If you have any objection to this, please let me know, but so many
of the poems in them have been reprinted elsewhere that I think
the time has come when we may let them become the prizes of
collectors. There are still left:

4 Copies of "Some Imagist Poets — 1915."
147 " " "Some Imagist Poets — 1916."
94 " " "Some Imagist Poets — 1917."

64

and you see it will not take very long at this rate before they are out of print. Most of the others of our little group have agreed to this, and if I do not hear from you on the subject I shall take it for granted that you have agreed with the rest of us to let the book go out of print. The price of printing is so high that I do not think the present sales justify keeping the volumes up.

I have no news; I wish I had. But everybody has gone to the war here just as they have with you, and travelling expenses are so high that people no longer travel round to meet each other as they used to. I suppose we must expect this, and certainly the war news is good.

I hope that you and Frieda are keeping well. I have heard nothing from any one in England except you for a long time. Do write from time to time. Stand not on the order of my letters, but write as the mood seizes you. I may be slow in my answers, but they will undoubtedly come.

With the very best of luck!

Sincerely yours,

34

Mountain Cottage
Middleton-by-Wirksworth
Derby.
11 Sept. 1918

My dear Amy,

I have today received your letter with the little cheque for the anthologies: the other letter I had a few days ago. — About the anthologies, you certainly know best. — Thank you for saying the nice things about me, in your essay.

Martin Secker is doing the poems which I inscribed to you: a small half-crown volume called "New Poems." I am expecting proofs now: the book should be out in six weeks' time. Secker will send you copies. I hope you'll like the book — or some of the things in it, at least.

Today I heard from Robert Nichols — you will have read his "Ardours and Endurances."[70] He is coming to America, lecturing on poets. You will see him — he is a friend of mine.

I haven't seen Hilda or Fletcher for a long time. Hilda has left Cornwall, and even had some idea of coming to America, I believe. But I don't expect she will. — Richard is still all right — in France, back of the firing lines.

I got the copy of "Poetry" with a notice on me by Fletcher[71] — very nice of him to take the trouble. When you are writing Harriett Monroe, thank her from me, will you, and please give her this address of mine.

Frieda and I are here trying to be patient. I am slowly working at another novel:[72] though I feel it's not much use. No publisher will risk my last, and none will risk this, I expect. I can't do anything in the world today — am just choked. — I don't know how on earth we shall get through another winter — how we shall ever find a future. Humanity as it stands, and myself as I stand, we just seem mutually impossible to one another. The ground dwindles under one's feet — what next, heaven knows.

I wish we could see you.

warm greetings

D. H. Lawrence

35

Mountain Cottage
Middleton by Wirksworth. Derby.
23 Sept. 1918

My dear Amy

I send you the proofs of the poems. I expect the book will be out in a month's time. You will get a copy.

Perhaps Harriett Monroe would care to publish some of these verses: if she would it would mean a few dollars — or if anyone else would do them. I don't know if my agent has arranged for American publication. I'll ask him.

Let me know how you like these. Write to us.

D. H. Lawrence

D. H. Lawrence, Esq.,
Mountain Cottage,
Middleton by Wicksworth,
Derby, England.
October 4, 1918.

Dear Lawrence:—

I shall be delighted to see your book of poems, and as I told you
in my last letter, I shall be extremely proud to see my name in
the dedication. I am sorry you are so blue. I know how hard it is,
and I know there is no use in counselling you to make any concessions to public opinion in your books; and, although I regret
sincerely that you cut yourself off from being published by an
outspokenness which the English public does not understand, I
regret it not in itself, as I think I said in my remarks about you
in that lecture, but simply because it keeps the world from
knowing what a great novelist you are. I think that you could top
them all if you would be a little more reticent on this one subject.
You need not change your attitude a particle, you can simply use
an India rubber in certain places, and then you can come into your
own as it ought to be. But what is the use? You will turn from
these remarks with a shrug of disgust and say, "Another, another,
they are all against me!" Of course that is not true, and of course
you must know that I do not mean it that way, but when one is
surrounded by prejudice and blindness, it seems to me that the only
thing to do is to get over in spite of it and not constantly run foul
of these same prejudices which, after all, hurts oneself and the
spreading of one's work, and does not do a thing to right the
prejudice. Few people are pure enough minded to take your books
as you mean them, which I tried to point out in my essay. I wish
that I could have made that essay on you longer, but you remember
that you never sent me any biographical material, and when Frieda
finally wrote me the thing had already been written and delivered.

I am sending you my new book. I do not know whether you will
like it or not. Sometimes I think you will not. You see, this poetry
is entirely objective, and you rather like the subjective kind.
However, such as it is it has gone to you, and I do hope that you
and Frieda will like some of it. At any rate, tell me just what you
think of it, please.

I will write again before long. In the meanwhile, with kindest regards to Frieda from Mrs. Russell and myself,

Very sincerely yours,

P.S. I think the war looks better, and some day we may all meet again.

37

Chapel Farm Cottage
Hermitage
nr. Newbury
Berks.
5 Nov. 1918

My dear Amy,

I have received Can Grande's Castle. You are wrong when you say I only like subjective poetry—I love visions, & visionary panorama. I love "thunderheads marching along the sky-line"— and "beautiful, faded city"—and "fifty vessels blowing up the Bosphorus"—and English Coaches—all those things. I love the pomp and richness of the past—the full, resplendent gesture. The sordidness of the present sends me mad—such meagre souls, all excusing themselves.—But why don't you write a *play*? I'm sure you could write a handsome drama.[73] Pity we can't do it together.—I do wish we could have some rich, laughing, sumptuous kind of days, insouciant, indifferent to everything but a little good laughter and splendeur de vivre which costs nothing.—Why not, one day.—Meanwhile as it happens to be a very sunny day, and the war will soon end, I feel already like a holiday.

No, Amy, again you are not right when you say the india-rubber eraser would let me through into a paradise of popularity. Without the india-rubber I am damned along with the evil, with the india-rubber I am damned among the disappointing. You see what it is to have a reputation. I give it up, and put my trust in heaven. One needn't trust a great deal in anything, & in humanity not at all.

I too have written a play:[74] not wicked but too good is probably the sigil of its doom. Que m'importe! I go my own way, regardless. By good I mean "sage:" one of my unspotted "sagesses."[75]

We went to London, Frieda & I—got the Flu.—fled here—have
recovered—shall probably return soon to Middleton. I have one
really passionate desire—to have wings, only wings, and to fly
away—far away. I suppose one would be sniped by anti-aircraft
guns. But one could fly by night. Then those indecent search-lights
fingering the sky.

Frieda sends her love. Remember us warmly to Mrs Russell.

D. H. Lawrence

38

Mountain Cottage
Middleton by Wirksworth
Derby.
28 Dec 1918.

My dear Amy

Why haven't we heard from you for so long? Did you ever get
my "New Poems"? You have not written since October, I believe,
not since you sent Can Grande.

Christmas is over now, and we must prepare for a new year. I
hope it will be a real new year, a new start altogether. The old has
been bad enough.—I was in London in November—saw Richard,
who was on leave. He is very fit, looking forward to peace and
freedom. Hilda also is in town—not so very well. She is going to
have another child, it appears. I hope she will be all right. Perhaps
she can get more settled, for her nerves are very shaken: and
perhaps the child will soothe her and steady her. I hope it will.

England is wintry and uncongenial. Towards summer time, I
want to come to America. I feel I want to be in a new country.
I expect we shall go to Switzerland or Germany when Peace is
signed. Frieda wants to see her people. Her brother-in-law is now
Minister of Finance to the Bavarian republic, one of my friends
is something else important, and F's cousin—Hartman von
Richthofen, whom they turned out of the Reichstag six months
ago, because he wanted peace—he is now a moving figure in
Berlin.[76] So Germany will be quite exciting for us. But I want to
come to America. I don't know why. But the land itself draws me.

We shall see you then. What are you doing in the meantime?—

are you coming over here? And why haven't you written a line. Remember us to Mrs Russell. A good New Year to you.

Yrs

D. H. Lawrence

39

Mountain Cottage
Middleton by Wirksworth
Derby
5 Feby. 1919

My dear Amy

I heard from Harriett Monroe that you did not receive the two copies of "New Poems" which Secker sent you. I am sorry. He is sending you now another copy.

You have not written at all since you sent "Can Grande" in the autumn — nor answered my letters. — By the way, is Can Grande's castle the Della Scala palazzo in Verona? — Can Grande was a Della Scala, I believe.[77] — It is very cold here. We have both been ill. I want spring & summer, terribly.

Will you come to Europe? I shall probably manage to come to America in the Summer. Let us have a word from you.

mila saluti buoni

D. H. Lawrence

40

D. H. Lawrence, Esq.,
Mountain Cottage,
Middleton by Wicksworth,
Derby, England.
17 February, 1919.

Dear Lawrence:—

Your letter of the 28th of December makes me realize very forcibly the fact that I have not written for so long; but the truth is that I have been very ill with the influenza, and although I did not die nor come anywhere near it, I have been too ill to do anything at all, and it left me exceedingly weak. You know what the thing is.

I have never received the copy of the book of poems which you say you sent me, and which is the reason I have not sent one to Harriet Monroe. I did get the proofs[78] and was very much pleased indeed to receive them, and I might have copied some of these poems and sent them to her; but, as you told me the book was coming, I thought it would be easier and simpler to wait for it, in case there were any changes. I do not know what happened to the book. It must have gone down, for I have never received it.

I am honoured to have these poems dedicated to me, and do hope you will send me the volume, although I really am more proud of having the book in proof; and I have no doubt my heirs will regard this as one of the most important items of my library.

The book itself interests me extremely, although I am bound to say it is not as overwhelming as "Look! We Have Come Through." You always manage to get tremendous feeling into your poems, and really a passion and emotion which fills me with envy and admiration. Your rhymes trouble me sometimes, but that may be idiosyncratic on my part.

Now let me tell you what I especially like in the book. I like "From a College Window." I like your expression of the pavements as "Summer white." How amusing it is to find you writing a triolet in "Bird Cage Walk." How did you ever think of that? Then I like "Flat Suburbs," with your "pink young houses" "flatly assuming the sun." Your "Letter from Town" also pleases me very much, and the last line of the first stanza is particularly nice. "Hyde Park at Night" is very good, particularly the first stanza, which I like immensely, and the last one; and as to "Gipsy," I am not sure that it is not the best thing in the book. "Two-Fold" is to me very interesting, but I am afraid the general public will see only the "bat" and "vat" rhymes, and they may smile. Not that you care, of course, but still—

"Under the Oak" is your old passion; and the mastery in it! That is the kind of poem which you do best, I think; and you cannot think how amusing and delightful it is to me to find in "Palimpsest of Twilight" that you too like night-scented stock. I wish you could see my garden in Summer. I have planted a mass of them, and it is glorious with perfume. And the fire-flies on a Summer's night! How you would write of them!

You have returned to the old subject of the dourness of death, as only you can do it, in "Bitterness of Death." Ah, but that poem is excellent and horrible! How the subject of death obsesses you, and how you show your Northern breeding in this cold and magnificent attitude. "Seven Seals" comes under the same head, I think, and is very fine. I like "Reading a Letter" very much, particularly the last two lines. They make everything so desolate.

Harriet Monroe writes me that it is not necessary now to send her anything, as she is in direct communication with you on the subject. If, however, you prefer to have me send her some of these poems, I will do so at once. There will be plenty of time for you to let me know, as she has just published some of your poems and therefore will not publish any more for a few months, I imagine.

What you tell me about Hilda is very interesting, and I hope the child will live, this time. I think that will make all the difference to her happiness. But she seems so frail, I cannot help fearing the outcome both for her and for the child.

It will be most interesting for you and Frieda to go abroad after the war, but when will it be "after the war"? Truly, the world seems terribly upheaved at present, and one cannot see a step in advance. I am very anxious to go to England to give some lectures on poetry, but I am strongly advised by everyone that this Summer will be too soon, and things will not have settled down sufficiently by then to make it possible to interest people in such a subject as poetry. So I suppose I shall have to wait until the Summer of 1920.

I hope you will come to America, but I think you may find it disappointing. It is far from being Eldorado, but there is no doubt whatever that the opportunity for writing is much greater here. There are many more magazines and enterprising editors, and the royalties are a great deal better, although the cost of living is a great deal higher, to match.

We still have royalties on our anthologies, which have not yet gone entirely out of print, and I am sending you your share. The account is as follows:

By Sales:

30 Imagist Poets, 1915		.36¼	10.88
17 " " 1916		.36¼	6.16
34 " " 1917		.36¼	13.32
10 do. 1915 to Eng.	.37½ less 15% Publishers		3.64
10 do. 1916 " "	.37½ less 15% Commission		3.64
	1/6 of		$ 37.64

is $6.27 or £1.5.7

This is not much of a letter, but, really, after being in bed for two months, I have not much to say. I wish I could see you and Frieda. Mrs. Russell joins me in very best wishes for the New Year. Do write and tell me how Hilda gets on, and above all things, do not wait for letters to answer, for if I do not answer yours promptly it is usually because something untoward has occurred which I cannot help. You cannot think how homesick I am to see you all in England.

Very sincerely yours,

41

Mountain Cottage, Middleton-by-Wirksworth, Derby. England.
5 April 1919.

My dear Amy

I am sorry you have been so seedy—one gets so pulled down. I had Flu—also—nearly shuffled off the mortal coil—am well on in convalescence. It was a vile sick winter for us all.— Hilda also had pneumonia some weeks ago, & it left her weak. I hear her baby, a girl, was born last Sunday, and that both are doing well. We shall be going to London soon, & may see her.

I am sure you are wise to defer your lectures on poetry—but I wish you were coming over to Europe. One feels a great longing for a bit of a gathering of friends in some sunny, careless, genial place. But the world is all at cross purposes, and gets worse: everything seems tangled in everything by a million bits of string. I want to go to Switzerland or Germany, and then come on to America this summer. But I can see we shall never manage it. I want awfully to come to America—first to the north, then later to go south, perhaps to Central America. It is what I intend to do when the world becomes sane again, and oneself free.

Here in England nobody cares about anything, literature least of all: all bent on scrambling uneasily from day to day, as if we were all perched on a land-slide, and the days were stones that might start sliding under one's feet. I don't know why it all seems so uncertain, so irritable, such a sequence of pinpricking moments, with no past to stay one, and no future to wonder over. But it is so. And it is hateful to have life chopped up into disagreeable moments, all gritty.

We hear from Frieda's people: terrible distress there seems to be. F. worries—we all worry. I suppose it will soon end. My brother-in-law is Minister of Finance to the new Bavarian republic. He seems to weather the storms. But it is a perpetual question of what next.—We want to go to Munich when we can. Frieda wants to see her mother and her sisters: I too want to see them all again.

When you write will you address me at—Chapel Farm Cottage, *Hermitage*, nr. *Newbury*, Berks. We are going down there at the end of the month, and I suppose we shall stay there till we leave England. I have not written anything these last few months—not since I have been ill. I feel I don't want to write—still less do I want to publish anything. It is like throwing one's treasures in a bog.

I agree with you, that the poetry of the future, and the poetry that *now* has the germs of futurity in it, is rhymeless, naked, spontaneous rhythm. But one has an old self as well as a new.—I hope you got the copy of New Poems. It was much better received than "Look we have Come Through." The press only spat on that.— What is Huebsch publishing of mine in New York, do you know? I never hear anything.

I do hope you are well & happy. I would love to see your garden, particularly to get the scents at evening. I would love the gorgeous, living lavishness that America is capable of, naturally—and Europe isn't.

Remember us to Mrs Russell. Frieda and I send warmest greetings.

D. H. Lawrence

42

Dear Amy,

I had a letter from Huebsch the other day, about the publishing of the poems etc. He seems very nice. He said he would arrange for me to lecture in America. I am not bent on lecturing, but don't mind if it *must* be done. I am making every arrangement possible to come to New York in August or September. I want very badly to come — to transfer myself. Huebsch said you told him you didn't think Boston would be the place for me to lecture in. Are you shy of me? — a little doubtful of the impression I shall, or should make? I hope not. I believe you are the only person I know, actually, in America, so I was hoping you'd help me a bit to find my feet when I come. Anyhow, tell me how you feel about it, won't you. — Probably I shall come alone, & Frieda will follow. If you don't want to be bothered — I admit it is a bother — just tell me. — I do hope your health is good now.

Have you any news? — any publications? I have nothing — except that I had some proofs of a little vol. of verse that C.W. Beaumont is hand-printing.[79] It is illustrated by absurd & unsuitable wood-cuts, by Anne Estelle Rice. Do you know her? She is American — one of the Matisse crowd from Paris — married a man called Drey. Well, her wood-cuts are silly, to my poems.

Here it is hot & dry. Summer has almost exploded into leaf this year; violence is really catching. We are waiting to be able to move. Frieda badly wants to go to see her people, but heaven alone knows when it will be possible.

I always hope to see you and have some happy times.

Remember us to Mrs Russell.

D. H. Lawrence

43

D. H. Lawrence, Esq.
Mountain Cottage,
Middleton by Wicksworth,
Derby, England.
10 June 1919.

Dear Lawrence:

I have two letters of yours to answer, one written on the 5th of April, and one, which I got this morning, on the 26th of May.

To answer the first one first, I am awfully sorry that you were so ill, but am glad to know that you are better now. Things are horrid, and this reconstruction period is very difficult to live through; there is no doubt about that.

Now as to your coming over to America. I am sorry Huebsch told you what I said about your coming to Boston, because undoubtedly he threw an entirely wrong light upon it. You need never doubt my loyalty, nor my anxiety to do everything I can for you and to push you in every way in my power. I have just reviewed "Look! We Have Come Through!" and it was printed on the first page of the "Times,"[80] that is, it was *the* review of the week, and Huebsch told me that it was responsible for selling out the first edition, so you see that I am doing everything I can for you. Huebsch also tells me that you have been writing articles for the English "Review" on American poets. I hope that you did not forget me in the process, but you do not mention it.

As to your lecturing here, you will not be angry with me, will you, if I tell you the exact truth of the situation as I see it?

The reason that I took this stand about Boston when Huebsch asked me if I could arrange for lectures for you here was because I know that to be an absolute impossibility. New England is far more puritanical than Old England. It is the most puritanical corner of this country. We have had a great many travelling Englishmen lecturing on a great many subjects, and a great many English poets, and I do not think that there is the same interest in that sort of thing that there was two or three years ago. Also, there was a great deal of clamour made over the suppression of your "Rainbow," and I am afraid that the feeling runs so high here that there would not be any chance of getting any lecture you might give well attended. Lectures cannot be given out of a blue sky. They

76

have to be under the auspices of a college or a woman's club, or run by an agent like the Pond Lecture Bureau. If Pond would take you on, it would be the best thing for you, but I doubt his doing it, as he has lost a great deal of money with various English poets lately. There are not enough learned foundations to make it worth while to consider them as an independent source of income, although they might be worked in if you had enough other lectures, but I doubt whether you could get any of them anyway. Women's Clubs, at any rate in this part of the country, are quite out of the question. It is unfortunate that the erotic side of your work has been too greatly stressed here, and real understanding of it is so rare. It is this point that I tried to bring out in my review, as you will see, but I am afraid that most of the world is too coarse-fibred to understand you. Now don't misunderstand me. I sympathize with you in every particular, and understand you and what you are trying to say perfectly. I know that there exists no more high-minded nor fine character in literature, but you have been misrepresented badly here, and I am afraid that that is going to dog you in the matter of getting lectures. Honestly, I do not believe that there is a chance for you anywhere in New England on the lecture platform. If I thought there was a possibility of doing anything for you in that way, you must know that I should be the first person to do it. America is in many ways far more backward and prudish than England, strange as it may seem. In a library, which I had occasion to go to the other day looking up a paper, I found most of Mr. Cannan's, Mr. Beresford's, and Mr. Mackenzie's books in the locked room as not fit for general circulation.[81] I also found there, to my horror, your "Sons and Lovers." Now if a superb volume like that is not considered proper to put into the hands of the public, what can you think of the attitude over here? I do not know whether that is true of other parts of the country in the same way at all, but it is perfectly true of this little corner of it.

It will be the greatest pleasure for me to see you personally; I long to have the talks of which you speak, and I long to see you and Frieda again, and Mrs. Russell joins me with the utmost cordiality, but I am afraid that you will find America a very different place from what you imagine, and what will be disgusting to you, as it is to me, is that they cannot see the difference between envisaging life whole and complete, physical as well as spiritual, and pure obscenities like those perpetrated by James Joyce.

I say nothing about nationality, because that depends very largely on the particular city in America in which you happen to be, but of course you are known to have married a German, and that is particularly difficult again in New England. I do not think that it would have the same effect in some of the cities of the middle West, such as Chicago or Cincinnati.

I tell you this merely that you may see what you are coming to, and I do think that it would be well for you to come here and see how the land lies yourself, but you must not look for El Dorado, because it is anything but that. Personally, I like it better here. I think that we have a truer feeling for values, and a grander conception of life, and a higher idea of art, even if we do not always get it on paper. But for people to understand what your books mean, they will have to see and know you, and for that reason I think it would be a good thing for you to come over, but I do not think it would be possible to get you any large quantity of lectures until you have made yourself known in other ways. When I told this to Huebsch he said: "But the man has got to live," and that is undoubtedly true, but I cannot think that the lecture platform will be anything but a disappointment to you, although it depends a good deal upon what Mr. Heubsch can get for you in New York and the West; I know that there is nothing here. Robert Nichols has been here all Winter, and although he may come back with glowing accounts of his success, I fear he exaggerates it, for he made no sort of an impression here, and was not liked personally, as I know you would be. I only refer to him as he had only two lectures, so far as I know, in this part of the country, one at Wellesley College and one before some Woman's Club.

There is a mistaken and ridiculous prejudice against your books, and that is the long and short of it; because it is undeserved it makes me want to weep. I think you are a big enough fellow to know that I write you a letter like this because I want you to know the facts of the case as they really are. If I cared less for you, I should put you off with some platitude. No one who knows you can fail to understand you, but it is almost impossible to make the general public understand, particularly when your books are prejudicial to their preconceived notions.

I hope Huebsch is going to publish your "New Poems." I urged him to when I saw him at the Booksellers' Convention a month ago. Those, I think, could circulate perfectly well.

Most of the radical magazines have been killed out by the war, and those that are left are all decidedly conservative, and that makes even journalism difficult. The situation is not easy all over the world. In some ways I think that it is harder in England than here, but I do advise you, if you can, to come over and see for yourself, for I know that you will make friends, and that is the most important thing in every branch of life. And you must understand that it would only be a pleasure and a delight to me to see you. Please always believe in my friendship, for it is most sincere.

Mrs. Russell is in Salt Lake City, or she would join me in kindest greetings to you and Frieda. Be sure and let me know when you come.

Sincerely yours,

44

Chapel Farm Cottage
Hermitage nr. Newbury
Berks. England
3 July 1919

My dear Amy

This morning comes your long letter. I do understand & believe perfectly what you say: particularly about lecturing. As for an El Dorado, when I set out to look for one, I shall find one: for nothing is easier to find than money, if a man sets out straight for it. I don't want El Dorado: only life and freedom, a feeling of bigness, and a radical, even if pre-conscious sympathy. I don't want to lecture — never did. I only want to be able to live. And I believe that, once in America, I could soon do that by writing. All I want is to feel that there is somewhere I could go, if necessary, and somebody I could appeal to for help if I needed it. That's why I am afraid of putting a burden on your friendship.

Huebsch said he was coming to England early this month. I am going to London today to see about things — a passport for Frieda, etc. She will go to Germany to her people quite soon: this month, I hope. I shall come to America, because I mean to come. Probably I shall sail in August. I shall come alone, Frieda will stay in Germany till I am a bit settled, then I shall send for her.[82] — I am not afraid of prejudices: they are rarely in the very blood, only in the mind, on top.

I want to feel that I may come to you, to stay with you for a week or two, if I can't provide for myself just at the very first. Don't fear, I can soon get on my own feet. It is merely the start.

My articles in the English Review were on *Classic* American Literature. I hope to do a series on the moderns, next.

Anyhow & anyway, I shall be seeing you soon—quite soon. The wind blows that way. Then we can have a laugh and many a talk.

D. H. Lawrence

45

D. H. Lawrence, Esq.
Chapel Farm Cottage,
Hermitage nr. Newbury,
Berks, England.
13 August 1919.

Dear Lawrence:

Your letter of July 3rd came a little while ago. I am very glad indeed to know that you are coming to America, but I do not know at all whether you will find it a pleasant place to work in. I hardly dare say you will; in fact, I am very much afraid you will not like it.

You may be quite sure that I shall do everything for you that I can. I can give you introductions to a great many publishers and editors, and I have already done my best to push your work, as you know.

Now here is the only difficulty with your plan. I cannot have people stay in the house with me. I am not at all strong, and I find it makes me very nervous to have guests, even delightful and intimate guests like yourself. Therefore, I have to make a rule of not having any one stay.

It is also a regrettable fact that Boston will not be a good place for your purpose. There are a few magazines here, and the only considerable one, "The Atlantic," is so old-fashioned and queer that I doubt whether they would care for your work. The field for you is distinctly New York, which is sad for me because I should like to feel that my town would be the one for you to settle in, but certainly the place for you to make connections with publishers and editors is New York. I should think, however, that it might be a good idea for you to come on here for a little while, either in the beginning or the middle of your stay in New York. At any rate, I shall see you much better in that way as I only go to New York occasionally. I shall be in New York lecturing the first of November, so that if you do not come there until then, I shall see you there.

I wish that so many of the radical papers had not been suppressed during the war. That has been a great trouble. The "Seven Arts," which was always sympathetic to your work, has gone under. I can, however, give you a letter of introduction to Louis Untermeyer, who was one of the editors, and he ought to be able to introduce you to the "Liberator" and various other magazines with which I have little to do. I can also give you introductions to "The Bookman," which is also George H. Doran Company who do publishing; to Knopf, another publisher; the Macmillans; Scribner's; "The Century"; "Harpers' "; "The Touchstone"; "The Independent"; "The North American Review"; and in Boston I can introduce you to Houghton Mifflin Company, and "The Atlantic." I could also send you a letter to Christopher Morley of the "Philadelphia Ledger," and to the magazine editor of the New York "Tribune," to the editor of the Literary Supplement of the "Times," and I can introduce you here to the "Transcript." I think these ought to be able to get you something. But, of course, people are terribly stocked; there is no doubt about it. The trouble would be that a good many of these papers pay on publication, and it would be a little while before the pay begins.

Chicago might be a better place for you than New York in the long run, but that you can decide when you get here. I know none of the newspaper editors in Chicago except the literary editor of the Chicago "News"; and, of course, Harriet, whom you know as well as I do. She could give you any introductions there.

By the way, I should have added "The New Republic" to my New York list and also "The Dial." I can give you introductions to both of them.

Of course your work is known in most radical circles, but not as much as it should be. You must be prepared to find the whole attitude toward literature in America entirely different from what it is in England, not perhaps in the way of being freer; it is more breezy, cruder perhaps. It is more liked by the man in the street. It requires rather a knack to write for American papers at first, but the pay is very good. The only trouble is that living expenses are very high, I should think perhaps three times as high as they are in England for everything.

You cannot imagine how anxious I am to see you and how much I look forward to the pleasant talks we ought to have, but really, to be strictly honest, I do not advise you to come at all. I wish that I could urge you to, but I cannot personally undertake to be responsible for you financially since the taxes occasioned by the war have cut very seriously into my income, and I cannot take on any more responsibility at present. I do not believe that you have the slightest idea of the price it costs to live in America. I have been making some inquiries and find that you cannot lodge and board in Boston for less than fifteen dollars a week and in New York for less than seventeen dollars a week. Everything has gone up here even more than it was before the war, and it has always been very high. Life is different here from what it is in England; it is stronger, harsher, and crueler, and, honestly, if I were you, I would not come. I fear that this may sound unkind; it is not intended to, and of course for me it would be the greatest pleasure to have you and Frieda in this country, but I am very much afraid that you will come here and find yourself stuck financially and cannot get home. I have been told that Wilfred Wilson Gibson[83] got so stuck in Chicago. I met a lady the other day who ran various readings and things for him to get enough money for him to go home. The only possible way in which an author can manage to live here, unless he is a very popular and rather trashy novelist, is to take a permanent job on some paper, reporting, or making-up, or something of that sort. Nobody attempts to live on their writing unless they have another job on the side, and it is very difficult indeed for an Englishman to get such a job in our Eastern cities. You know the Irish question is very rife at present, and that makes some difference. Also, it requires a good deal of knack and training to know exactly what newspapers want, and while you are acquiring this knack, even supposing you would be willing to take a permanent job, you must live. Mr. Huebsch may know of something better than I do for you, but I am connected with no paper and have no pull anywhere. All I can do is to give you introductions which will assure you of a courteous reception, but will guarantee nothing more.

I fear for you disappointment and disaster. It is a curious climate in this part of the country, and yet here is the place to make connections. If you place any value on my advice, you will understand the spirit in which I write this, and you will not attempt this vast and difficult country in your state of health.[84]

Mrs. Russell joins me in best wishes to you and Frieda.

Always very sincerely yours,

9, SELWOOD TERRACE,
SOUTH KENSINGTON, S.W.

11 August 1914

My Dear Miss Lowell,

It is very good or nice of
you to ask us to dinner on Thursday.
We look forward very much to coming.
I suppose I need n't dress — just as
you ordain. Is Mrs Russell staying
with you? — I did not know. My
respects to her, and it is a pleasure
to meet her again.

All my wails & laments I shall
pour out when I come

Küss' die Hand

D. H. Lawrence

Lawrence's note to Lowell, 11 August 1914
(Letter 2). Courtesy Houghton Library, Harvard University.

Higher Tregerthen, Zennor, St. Ives, Cornwall.
14 Novem. 1916

My dear Amy

I was infinitely touched when there came this morning a cheque for £60, sent by you through the bankers. One is so moved by the kindness: the money, after all, is necessity, but the kindness is given. This I shall always treasure up, the kindness, even if I can pay you back the money. Because after all, there is not much real generosity in the world.

I was rather sorry Frieda wrote and asked you for money: how do we know what you have to do with your money. But it is wearying, to be so much unwell, and penniless. I shall begin at once to move towards Italy: though heaven knows when we shall really get away. And I hope, from Italy, to come on to America, next year, when I am better and the winter has gone.

Why don't you come to Rome for a while? Think how jolly that would be, if we were all in Rome at the same time. Perhaps you would like it better, in these times, than London.

The first page of Lawrence's letter to Lowell, 14 November 1916 (Letter 22). Courtesy Houghton Library, Harvard University.

D. H. Lawrance, Esq.,
Mountain Cottage,
Middleton By Wicksworth,
Derby, England.

October 4, | 8.

Dear Lawrence:-

     I shall be delighted to see your book of poems, and as I told you in
my last letter, I shall be extremely proud to see my name in the dedication.
I am sorry you are so blue. I know how hard it is, and I know there is no
use in counselling you to make any concessions to public opinion in your
books; and, although I regret sincerely that you cut yourself off from being
published by an outspokenness which the English public does not understand,
I regret it not in itself, as I think I said in my remarks about you in that
lecture, but simply because it keeps the world from knowing what a great
novelist you are. I think that you could top them all if you would be a
little more reticent on this one subject. You need hot change your attitude
a particle, you can simply use an India rubber in certain places, and then
you can come into your own asit ought to be. But what is the use? You will
turn from these remarks with a shrug of disgust and say, "Another, another,
they are all against me!" Of course that is not true, and of course you must
know that I do not mean it that way, but when one is surrounded by prejudice
and blindness, it seems to me that the only thing to do is to get over in
spite of it and not constantly run foul of these same prejudices which, after
all, hurts oneself and the spreading of one's work, and does not do a thing
to right the prejudice. Few people are pure enough minded to take your books
as you mean them, which I tried to point out in my essay. I wish that I
could have made that essay on you longer, but you remember that you never
sent me any biographical material, and when Frieda finally wrote me the thing
had already been written and delivered.

     I am sending you my new book. I do not know whether you will like it
or not. Sometimes I think you will not. You see, this poetry is entirely

The first page of Lowell's letter to Lawrence, 4 October 1918 (Letter 36). Courtesy Houghton Library, Harvard University.

D. H. Lawrence from about 1915. Courtesy Bassano and Vandyke.

Amy Lowell from about 1920. Courtesy
Houghton Library, Harvard University.

Amy Lowell in her garden in 1922. Courtesy
Houghton Library, Harvard University.

D. H. Lawrence in the cloisters of Cuernavaca Cathedral in the spring of 1923. Photo by Witter Bynner. Courtesy Houghton Library, Harvard University.

The east end of Amy Lowell's library at Sevenels. Courtesy Houghton Library, Harvard University.

46

D. H. Lawrence, Esq.
Chapel Farm Cottage,
Hermitage Nr. Newbury,
Berks, England.
24 September 1919.

Dear Lawrence:

Here is our very small half-yearly royalty from Houghton Mifflin Company. As you know, we are letting the Anthologies go out of print, so that the royalties get smaller and smaller. The account is as follows:

	By sales:			
24	Imagist Poets, 1915		.43½	10.44
20	" " 1916		.43½	8.70
24	" " 1917		.43½	10.44
				$ 29.58

One-sixth of $29.58 is $4.93

I have not heard from you since I wrote you last. I do hope that you understood my letter. It is hard to make one's self really understood on paper, but I think you must know what a difficult letter it was for me to write, and it would not have been written had I not felt convinced that it was the only thing to do to tell you the situation just as it was.

I understand that Mr. Huebsch did not go to England. I do not know what he wrote you in regard to coming here, but I saw a very intimate friend of his the other day, and he told me that he had seen Mr. Huebsch, and Mr. Huebsch felt as I did, that the outlook was far from favorable for you.

I wonder if Frieda has gone to Germany. Do write when you have time and tell me how things are with you. I hope to go over to England next Spring, but that will depend on the conditions of all our countries.

I shall send you my new book in a few days.[85] I trust that there will be something in it that you will like.

Please remember me most kindly to Frieda, and believe me,

Very sincerely yours,

83

47

[Postcard]
5. Piazza Mentana. Florence.
26 Novem. [1919]

My dear Amy—

I have not thanked you for your letters, which were really kind, and which I understood. I have come to Italy for the winter—Frieda is coming down from Baden-Baden next week, to join me here, then we are going further South.—I have a room here over the Arno, which is noisy and swollen with rain. The war has left its mark on people here too—but not so much. There is still some blessed *insouciance* in the Italians. I wonder how you are. Send me a line.

D. H. Lawrence

48

D. H. Lawrence, Esq.
5 Piazza Mentane
Florence, Italy.
9 January 1920.

Dear Lawrence:

Thank you ever so much for your letter of November 26th from Florence. It is good to know that you understood my letters. Indeed you need never doubt my friendship nor my desire to help you nor my admiration of your superb work.

I am enclosing a draft for one hundred dollars as a New Year's gift which may come in handy on your trip. I wonder if Gilbert Cannan ever sent you any money. He told he was collecting from various friends for you. He seems to have your welfare at heart, but he did not seem to me to know you very intimately.

I do hope that the Winter will do both you and Frieda lots of good. I am facing another operation, since the one I had a year and a half ago has not been an entire success.[86] It is an awful nuisance and cuts into my work badly. Shall you go back to London this Spring? I have no idea when I shall go there. It depends somewhat on my work and a great deal on conditions in England. Every one there tells me that is useless to think of going there now and that the living there is most uncomfortable.

I have at last found an enthusiastic English publisher in Basil Blackwell, so that I hope my work may generally come to be known. The Macmillans did nothing with it, neglected to supply it when it was asked for by booksellers and things of that sort.

I hear from Richard Aldington with some frequency, but not as often as I could wish. Do write to me every now and then and let me know how you and Frieda are and where you are. I trust this letter will never reach you; if you do get it let me know. Of course it is much more important that you should let me know if you do not get it, but I fail to see how I can convey that information to you.

With the best of good wishes for the New Year, and many of them,

Very sincerely yours,

49

Palazzo Ferraro
Capri
Prov. di Napoli.
Italy.
13 February 1920

My dear Amy

Today I have your letter, and cheque for thirteen-hundred Lire. How very nice of you to think of us this New Year. But I wish I needn't take the money: it irks me a bit. Why can't I earn enough, I've done the work. After all, you know, it makes one angry to have to accept a sort of charity. Not from you, really, because you are an artist, and that is always a sort of partnership. But when Cannan writes and tells me he has collected a few dollars — which, of course, I have not received — he wrote me to tell me he was collecting a few, but never wrote again. Cannan annoys me, with his sort of penny-a-time attempt at benevolence, and the ridiculous things he says about me — & everybody else — in the American press.[87] I am a sort of charity-boy of literature, apparently. One is denied one's just rights, and then insulted with charity. Pfui! to them all.— —But I feel you & I have a sort of odd congenital understanding, so that it hardly irks me to take these Liras from you, only a little it ties me up. However, one must keep ones trust in a few people, & rest in the Lord.

I am extremely sorry you are not well, and must have an operation. Such a thought is most shattering. Pray to heaven it won't hurt much & will make you right.— Blackwell is a good publisher for getting at the young life in England. He's much more in touch with the future, than old Macmillan.

Secker has done another edition of my *New Poems*, properly bound now.[88] I shall have him send you a copy. I asked Beaumont to send you a copy of a tiny book of mine "Bay," which he has handprinted.[89] He is not very responsible — tell me if you have received it.

No, don't go to England now, it is so depressing and uneasy and unpleasant in its temper. Even Italy isn't what it was, a cheerful insouciant land. The insouciance has gone.[90] But still, I like the Italians deeply: and the sun shines, the rocks glimmer, the sea is unfolded like fresh petals. I am better here than in England.— Things are expensive, and not too abundant. But one lives for the same amount, about, as in England: and freer to move in the air and over the water one is, all the while. Southwards the old coast glimmers its rocks, far beyond the Siren Isles. It is very Greek — Ulysses ship left the last track in the waves. Impossible for Dreadnoughts to tread this unchangeable morning-delicate sea.

Frieda came down to Florence from Germany: a bit thinner & wiser for her visit. Things are wretchedly bad there. I must have food sent all the time to F's mother from England, & for the children — there absolutely isn't enough to eat.

We have got two beautiful rooms here at the top of this old palace, in the very centre of Capri, with the sea on both hands. Compton Mackenzie is here — a man one can trust and like, which — as far as the first goes — is more than one can say of Cannan.— But Capri is a bit small, to live on. Perhaps I shall go to the mainland — perhaps not. Anyway this address will always find me.— I have just begun a new novel.[91]

I feel we shall see you in Italy. I do hope you will be better. Is Mrs Russell with you always? A thousand greetings from both.

D. H. Lawrence

50

D. H. Lawrence, Esq.
5 Piazza Mentane
Florence, Italy.
1 March 1920.

My dear Mr. Lawrence:

Miss Lowell has recently undergone an operation, and while she is getting on famously she is not yet able to do any work, so I am enclosing you the draft for the semi annual Imagist Royalties.

Yours very truly,

Secretary.

51

Fontana Vecchia
Taormina
Prov. di Messina. Sicily.
9 March. 1920

Dear Amy

My bank, Haskard & Co. of Florence, where I have a little account, sent me the enclosed letter about the 1315 Lire which you gave me. I don't know why the Credito Italiano is fussing. But stop the cheque at your bank, will you, lest they swindle us. — It is always easiest to have a cheque made out in dollars — they give much more for it here. For $100 I can sometimes get Lire 1800, which pays my rent for nearly the whole year: a vast consideration. — Only don't let us *both* be done out of the money.

We have come here, and taken such a lovely house in a garden, for a year. It costs 2000 L. It is really lovely. Only travelling is so trying and so expensive.

There are real good hotels here. If you are well enough, perhaps you will come, during the course of our year.

I do wish you felt well & strong. Tell me if you get the various books I have ordered to be sent to you.

Italy feels shaky—Europe altogether feels most insecure. There'll be another collapse soon. Mais à la guerre comme à la guerre.[92]

Send me a line to say how you are.

D. H. Lawrence

52

D. H. Lawrence, Esq.
Fontana Vecchia
Taormina
Prov. di Messina
Sicily
29 May 1920.

Dear Lawrence:

Here is your draft in English money. I have had an awful time because I had to buy back the old draft and pay $35.00 for the difference, and the bank tells me that they can see no reason why your bank should not have paid it. I cannot help thinking there is something funny somewhere about the way your bank behaved. However, here it is.

I wonder what you and Frieda are doing in Sicily. I wish I were with you. Here I am drowned in work and just about to start off on a trip down South to get the degree of Doctor of Literature,[93] which sounds very fine and means nothing at all. Things are going on much the same here. I see your poems from time to time. I think the last I saw were in "Coterie" or "Voices."[94] I am not much impressed by either of those magazines, but I am glad they have the sense to have you in them. Forgive haste, I am hurrying to get off.

Very sincerely yours,

53

My dear Amy

My landlord, a young Sicilian, is coming to Boston to be a cook, so he is bringing you this letter and this little ricordo.[95] He is Francesco Cacòpardo, called Cicio, and his address c/o Mr William B. Rogers, Potter & Rogers, 3 Doane St., Boston, Mass. His young wife Emma is coming with him. I like them very much. He speaks good English.

I wonder if you are well — fear you aren't. I wrote you three months ago about the cheque for 100 dollars which you sent me for New Year, but I have no answer. The bank wouldn't cash the cheque — I haven't had it at all. I hope you stopped it at your bank, so that it is not just swindled away.

I have been very busy here at Taormina, and have finished a novel which I hope may get serialised, and then I shall be quite well off. Secker is to do it in England. He will also do The Rainbow again, and Women in Love, the sequel to The Rainbow. In New York Thomas Seltzer, of 5 West 50th Street, is doing a limited edition of Women in Love, 2 vols., 15 dollars — he says. I shall tell him to send you a copy, and I hope you'll like it, because I consider it my best novel. — Seltzer will also, I suppose, do the new novel *The Lost Girl*; but I want to get this serialised first, perhaps in The Century, which Secker suggests.[96]

We went to Malta, and it was so hot I feel quite stunned. I shouldn't wonder if my skin went black and my eyes went yellow, like a negro's. The south is so different from the north. I believe morality is a purely climatic thing.

The bougainvillia creeper is bright magenta, on the terrace here, and through the magenta the sea is dim blue and magical, summer-white. Nearly all the strangers have gone from Taormina, we are alone with the natives, who lie about the streets with a sort of hopeless indifference. Here the past is so much stronger than the present, that one seems remote like the immortals, looking back at the world from their otherworld. A great indifference comes over me — I feel the present isn't real.

The corn is already cut, under the olive orchards on the steep, sloping terraces, and the ground is all pale yellow beneath the almonds and the vines. It is strange how it is September among the earth's little plants, the last poppy falling, the last chicory flower withered, stubble and yellow grass and pale, autumn-dry earth: while the vines are green and powerful with spring sap, and the almond trees, with ripe almonds, are summer, and the olives are timeless. Where are we then?

We love our Fontana Vecchia, where we sit on our ledge and look far out, through the green, to the coast of Greece. Why should one travel — why should one fret? Why not enjoy the beautiful indifference. Earnestness seems such bad taste, with this coast in view.

But Frieda is a bit scared of the almighty sun. She hankers after Germany, after the Schwarzwald — fir-trees, and dewy grass. She makes plans that we shall go north to Baden in August, for a couple of months. But I don't know. It costs so much, to travel, and is such a horrible experience nowadays, particularly in Italy.

We send you two bits of Taormina work. The women sit in the streets all day long, and do it. It is what the loom was to the pagan women, Penelope or Phaedra. Only the pagan women were indoors in some upper room, while these women sit together in the street, week after week, year after year. In the south there is no housework: no one knows what a Hausfrau is. Soup is boiled at evening, when the light fades. While the long day lasts the women sit with their frames in the street, dark, palish, intent, rather like industrious conspirators, working and talking: a wee bit sinister, as pagan women always seem to me sinister.

The brown strip, Frieda says, is for a dress or coat or something: the cushion is amusing. I wonder how many hours of Taormina life they represent. The women are Greek here — not Italian: lean and intense. The coast is all Greek — Naxos buried just below us, Polyphemos' rocks in the sea way down.

Well, I hope your health is good, that's the chief thing. Your garden will be gorgeous now. We both send many good wishes. Remember me to Mrs Russell.

D. H. Lawrence

I send you a copy of my play.[97] Seltzer will send you another copy, which you can give away.

54

My Dear Amy

I had your letter with 100 dollar cheque three days ago: am very sorry about the cheque: wish you hadn't sent it again, but just cancelled the old one. — They robbed you: plainly robbed you. But the banks always do it. The Lira is up again, so I only got 1550 for the 100 dollars: but still *I* make, while you lose. Too bad. A while back I should have got 2500 Lire for 100 dollars. — I hope my affairs are going to come right before long: time they did: then I shall be able to help others, instead of being helped. Meanwhile, — touch wood! — I think I'm all solvent for the next year — according to my prospects.

So you are a Doctor by now: of Divinity I nearly said! And Shall one address you as Doctor Amy Lowell? — and "my dear Doctor —"? Well well — all titles seem to me comical: even Mr. & Miss & Mrs. I like my stark name best.

I wonder if Ciccio has arrived in Boston, & sent you the bits of Taormina work & my letter. You might even see him one day: he is a dear, so is Gemma. I'll tell you the romance of them. — Gemma & her family, with 1000 other refugees, were shipped down here from the Venetian province when the Austrians broke in. She was with her mother & nine brothers & sisters, barefoot, with nothing but a blouse & skirt, penniless. Ciccio fell in love with her: female half of Taormina enraged, for Ciccio is rich & speaks 3 languages. One irate woman attacked Gemma & tore the blouse off her back. The Mottas — Gemmas family — viewed Ciccio with wild suspicion & said he was going to make poor Gemma his concubine. Still they refused to believe he was married. So this time, before he left for Boston, he went up to the Veneto with his wife, & my heart, she was rigged up: silk stockings, suède shoes, georgette frock: she who had never worn a hat in her life till Ciccio bought her one: propria contadina.[98] I wish I could hear now how the visit to San Michele went off. I hope you are well and happy, mon cher Docteur.

D. H. Lawrence

55

D. H. Lawrence, Esq.,
Fontana Vecchia,
Taormina,
Prov. di Messina,
Sicily.
30 July 1920.

Dear Lawrence:

I have two letters of yours to answer, one of the first of June, and one of the twenty-sixth. I want to thank you for the beautiful embroideries which you and Frieda have sent. I cannot tell you how much I like them and how useful they will be. The strip of open-work linen is beautiful in colour, like crushed strawberries, and will look charmingly on a gown; and as to the cushion cover, it is exactly what I want and need most. I do think it was most kind of you two to think of this charming present, and I am extremely grateful.

I am just on the wing to Chicago where I am to give two lectures before the Summer School of the University of Chicago. When I come back I will look up your Sicilian, although I cannot see what good it will do as I am not by way of being able to employ him. However, I will certainly look him up, as I should so much like to hear from some one's lips how you are. I am glad to know that he speaks English, as I do not speak Italian.

I do not know whether I ever wrote you about your new book, "Bay." I think it the best volume of poems which you have printed so far, poetry, that is; for poignancy, I believe you will never outdo "Look! We Have Come Through," but for pure poetry, I think this new volume charming. I also got the copy of "Touch and Go" which you sent me, and which I have read with enormous interest. That preface is a masterpiece, and the whole play seems to me so true, so exactly the fact, everybody is wrong, everybody is pulling against everybody else. It is a ghastly time, I wish we lived in some other.

You will be glad, at least I hope you will be, to know that I am reviewing "Touch and Go" for the "New York Times." I am also taking a little shy in it at your preface to "New Poems" issued by Huebsch.[99] The book has already been reviewed by a man named Gorman, but I wanted to have a say about the preface, and they have permitted me to lug this into my review of "Touch and Go."

I have not read the preface thoroughly yet, I have only glanced at it. I rather think I shall disagree with you there, but I hope you won't mind.

I am awfully glad to know that you have got a new novel coming along, and I have taken the liberty of suggesting to the "Dial" that they go round and see Seltzer and try if they cannot secure it to print serially. The "Dial" has changed hands and is now being backed by a rich young man who pays very well and quite promptly.[100] They are interested in having material by well-known authors, and I think they will jump at your book, and I rather advise you to take their offer if they do, as the magazines here are so old fogy. The "Dial" is a little too futuristic for my taste, but it has life and vigour and a good clientèle, and I really cannot think of any other magazine here in which you would be better off. But I do not want you to take my advice if Mr. Seltzer is against it. I want you to know what I have done, for I always have your interest at heart, as you know.

It is too bad about the exchange having dropped before you got that cheque of mine. I wonder whether you are going to Germany or will stay in Sicily. I believe I love warm countries best. I have just been down to Texas where the thermometer was 106; I liked it but I am sorry to say that Mrs. Russell did not.

Again many thanks for the beautiful cushion cover and the lovely strip. Please give Mrs. Russell's and my love to Frieda.

Very sincerely yours,

56

D. H. Lawrence, Esq.
Fontana Vecchia,
Taormina
Prov. di Messina
Sicily.
12 August 1920.

Dear Lawrence:

Here is a draft for your share of the half-yearly royalties on the Imagist Anthologies.

By sales

20 Imagist Poets,	1915			.46⅔	$9.33
23	"	"	"	.58⅓	13.42
13	"	"	1916	.46⅔	6.07
17	"	"	"	.58⅓	9.92
19	"	"	1917	.46⅔	8.87
21	"	"	"	.58⅓	12.25
					$59.86

One sixth of $59.86 is $9.97

I have not time for more now as I am just taking the train to Chicago to give a couple of lectures, and I want this to go at once. Much love to Frieda from us both.

Very sincerely yours,

57

Florence.
12 Sept 1920

My dear Amy

I had your nice long letter a few days ago, in Venice. Glad you got the bits of embroidery, shall be amused to see your tilting against the New Poems preface. Agree with you about Bay. — You'll send me your review of Touch & Go?

Frieda wanted to go to Germany: has gone: so I have been wandering round Lake Como & Venice, & now am here for a while in an explosion-shattered, rambling old villa which a friend has lent me. It is hot, wine harvest has begun, the Italians cry out that they are persecuted like Job: what with earthquakes & manquakes.

F. talks of coming south again in early October when, I presume, we shall wander our way south to Taormina. We left in early August. It was *very* hot. I like warm countries, but it was too much for me, month after month. I sympathise with Mrs Russell.

Do you like Venice? I think it is so lovely to look at. I thought you were coming to Italy. Myriad Americans are here. With the exchange, it is cheap. All feels very fizzy & bubbly: but don't suppose anything big will happen—though it just might.—Why don't you trip over? Greet Mrs Russell.

D. H. Lawrence

I got the 9 dollars for Imagist—many thanks. I ought to dart & change them at 22/50.

58

Am back here waiting for Frieda, who comes in a day or two. Venice looking very charming—but a bit hollow, I feel her, poor old thing. Robert Mountsier is back in New York, and is looking after my affairs.[101] Do you know him? 417 West 118 Street. He's a friend. I've done a new little volume of *Vers Libre*—so queer.[102] Shall send Mountsier an MS. Should like to know what you think of it.

Yrs

D. H. Lawrence

59

Fontana Vecchia
Taormina
Sicily.
30 November 1920.

My dear Amy

I wonder how you are. Here we sit in Sicily & it has done nothing but rain masses of rain since we are back. But today a rainbow and tramontana[103] wind & blue sea, & Calabria such a blue morning-jewel I could weep. The colour of Italy is blue, after all. Strange how rare red is. But orange underglow in the soil & rock here.

95

The little rose cyclamens are almost over: the little white &
yellow narcissus are out among the rocks, scenting the air, and
smelling like the world's morning, so far back. Oranges are nearly
ripe, yellow and many — and we've already roasted the autumn kids:
soon it will be Christmas.

I had your review notice of *Touch & Go*. Did I thank you? I hope
you've got *Women in Love* from Seltzer: I asked him to send it you.
Of all my novels, I like it far best. But other people don't and won't.
Tell me *please* what you think. — I've ordered Secker to send you
also The Lost Girl, which is just out in London. Perhaps this will
sell, & make me some money. I don't think *Women in Love* will
sell.

I did a little book of vers libre — *Birds, Beasts, and Flowers:* am
awaiting it from the typist. Frieda hates it: I like it. *Songs without
Sound* I'd like to call them. When I get the MS. I think I shall send
it to you for your opinion, am so curious to know.

Haven't you got a new book?

We keep making plans for the Spring. I think I shall go to Germany for a time. Where are you going.

Greetings from both of us to you for Christmas.

D. H. Lawrence

Even if you don't like *Women in Love* very much, have a certain
gentle feeling towards it, because I ask you.

60

[From Ada Russell]
D. H. Lawrence, Esq.
c/o Frau Baronin von Richthofen,
Ludwig-Wilhelmstift,
Baden-Baden, Germany.
19 May 1921.

My dear Mr. Lawrence:

You will be awfully sorry to know that Amy had to undergo her
fourth operation. It happened Tuesday, the 17th, and the doctors
say they think that this one will really be successful; at any rate,
Amy says it is their last chance; her third one having been October

29th 1920, so you can realize why she has not been able to write with the press of work always at her back.

"Legends" is coming out this week, her book of narrative poems. Also, Mrs. Ayscough, her collaborator in China, arrived just before this last operation, and she worked against time correcting the poems[104] and so was very tired just before she had to give up. She wanted awfully to catch up with her mail but found it impossible.

She received the books: "Women in Love," "The Lost Girl," and just to-day arrived "Psychoanalysis and the Unconscious." Of course you know how much she admires your work always, it is unnecessary for me to tell you that, and I hope before long that she will be able to write it all out for herself.

I hope Frieda is well. We often talk of you and look forward to seeing you both again sometime in the future.

With best wishes, yours most sincerely

P.S. Since writing the above, Mr. Seltzer has sent us your address in Germany. The bank tells me that the only way they can send money to that country is through one in Berlin. The royalties for the Anthologies amount to $8.09, and if you will tell me what you would like done with it, it shall be attended to.

61

D. H. LAWRENCE, ESQ.
c/o Frau Baronin von Richthofen
Ludwig-Wilhelmstift,
Baden-Baden Germany.
6 July 1921

Dear Lawrence:

Your letter to Mrs. Russell came the other day, and I have at last got far enough to write to you with my own voice, if not my own hand. In spite of your sweetness in wanting me to buy a pot of fuchsias with your share of the Imagist royalties, I cannot feel justified in not forwarding it to you. There will be another pittance from the same source shortly, I suppose. The bond between us is intensified by your picking fuchsias, as they are one of my favourite flowers. I shall never forget how they used to hang over the walls of the house in Devonshire when I passed a Summer there years ago.

Your reputation is coming on here by leaps and bounds, I am happy to say. I did not place any of the poems in the last batch you sent because your agent in New York, Mr. Mountsier, seemed to think that that was his prerogative, and I thought he probably got a percentage on it and so did not like to butt in. I suggested making a try at it, but he made it so evident that he preferred to do it himself that I let it alone. I did, however, tell the editor of the "Bookman" that he ought to get your "Mosquito," and he did, and it appears in the current number of the magazine, as does also a little criticism of mine of your "Apostolic Beasts," which came out shortly before in "The Dial."[105] I would send you the number only I have my doubts about its following you about Europe and ever arriving.

I do not know when I was ever so interested in a book as I was in your "Women in Love." The scene on the lake, beginning with the wonderful beauty of the lanterns and ending with the horror of the drowning, was superb I thought. I confess I did not care as much for "The Lost Girl." It did not seem to be as truly you. I felt that you were modifying yourself to gain your public, which was undoubtedly a very wise thing to do, but I did not find the result as interesting. I could not review the book because of these perpetual operations which have made my life such a burden lately. I have had three in fifteen months, and it takes me months to get over each one, so I have had hardly any breathing space at all this year. I am in hopes that this last one will be final, but one never can tell. "The Lost Girl" has been excellently reviewed, however. I have read a great deal about it in a great many places. One of the best reviews has just appeared in the "Freeman" by Mrs. Padraic Colum,[106] who compares it with our great commercial success, Sinclair Lewis's "Main Street," much to the detriment of the latter.

I wish I saw a chance of our meeting before long, but I have not been allowed by the surgeons to cross the water for some time. I am hoping to get over to England next Spring, but again, who knows.

Brentano asked me to write a little notice of you for their advertising circular, a sort of biography and criticism in one, but I could not do it, I was too ill. Somebody else did it, I observe, and not at all badly.

Your description of Baden Baden sounds charming. Now that Harding has signed the Peace Treaty, I suppose the question of mail will not be so difficult. Do write and keep me in touch with all you are doing. I have seen nothing but my bedroom for weeks. Give both Mrs. Russell's and my love to Frieda, and forgive my long silence; you know it could not be helped.

Affectionately yours,

P.S. I am sending you a copy of my new volume, "Legends," I hardly know whether you will like it or not, but I trust, at any rate, that it will reach you.

62

[Postcard]
[Villa Alpensee, Thumersbach]
[Zell-am-See]
[20 or 21 July 1921]

We are leaving here this week for Florence —
32 Via dei Bardi
Suppose we shall stay there till end of September, then to Taormina again for the winter. Hope you are getting strong and feeling well, and having a good time with Legends notices.

Yrs.

D. H. Lawrence

63

[Postcard]
Thumersbach. Zell-am-See
30 July. [1921]

Today has come the copy of "Legends," forwarded from Baden Baden: for which many thanks. I shall read it this evening. We are here in Austria, in the Tyrol among the mountains for a while — very pleasant to see the snow looking fierce, and to hear the water roaring once more savage and unquenched. In Sicily water expires so soon. Here it is rampant and full of lust. — I hope you are better from all operations, and enjoying the launch abroad of *Legends*.

Frieda sends many greetings, with mine. Remember us to Mrs Russell. The Baden address is always safe.

D. H. Lawrence

64

**Villa Alpensee
Thumbersbach
Zell-am-See bei Salzburg
Austria
31 July 1921**

Dear Amy

I had your letter and the eight-dollars yesterday. I had much rather you had had the fuchsia tree. There are lovely ones here.

Very many thanks for looking after my poems so kindly. Mountsier is over here just now. He is rather overbearing, I fancy. I had understood that you had said, of the poems, that The Mosquito was the only one worth printing.

I do hope the operation was successful & final & that you can live your own life freely.

I read Legends last night, — and again this morning. I like them the best of all your poems. You have always written of the existence & magic of *things* — porcelain and rain: and of *things* you catch an essence: even cannon & ships. But in this book it is life and death superseding things. So I like this book the best.

I like best *Many Swans*[107] which I have read twice and which I feel really speaks inside my unexplained soul. I should not like to try to explain it, because of the deep fear and danger that is in it. But it isn't a myth of the sun. It is something else. All the better that we can't say offhand what. That means it is true. It rings a note in my soul. Then I like Blackbird & Witch Woman. But I doubt if you quite get her — the Witch Woman.

Those three, for me, are much the best, & the best of all your poems.

The Statue is very amusing & nicely done — only Julius got off too lightly. His *things* should have pinched him a bit more excruciatingly. She should have flung her leaden arms round his neck in the lake, & nothing but bubbles to tell the tale. I must read Yucca & Passion Vine again. I don't quite get it. But it is most *interesting*, after Swans. Porcelain is lovely as things.

I hope you'll have as much pleasure as you wish out of the public reception of the book.

Wonder what you'll do next.

D. H. Lawrence

65

D. H. Lawrence, Esq.
c/o Frau Baronin Von Richthofen
Ludwig-Wilhelmstift
Baden-Baden, Germany.
7 September 1921

Dear Lawrence:

I wonder if you have the slightest idea of how much pleasure your letter about "Legends" has given me. I know what you mean by my insistence on *things*. My things are always, to my mind, more than themselves, but I do believe I have laid too much insistence upon them, and obscured the more important issues beneath them for my readers. I am trying not to do this now except in poems that are apparently only things, and that you see what you do in "Many Swans" makes me very happy, because it was exactly what I tried to put into that poem. Sometimes I wonder whether I shall live long enough, and grow enough, to be able to put into my poetry what I want to have there. I don't know, one can only live and try to go on growing. The technique of poetry is easy, very easy to any one born that way; life is not easy, and it is still less simple to express in words the real throb, and misery, and gusto which it has. That is what you do, and that is what I wish I could learn of you.

I never said that "The Mosquito" was the only one of the poems of that batch that was worth printing. I do not know who could have so misrepresented me. I thought "The Turkey-cock" superb. I am enclosing a few remarks I made on "The Apostolic Beasts," which may interest you. Your whole "Tortoise" set was magnificent, but I feared the public would misunderstand them and fall

101

upon you with renewed vigour. The public is a mole, a blind, blundering bat. I have written about you again and again, and tried to get it into people's heads what you are, what you are striving for, and I do believe things are moving at last.

By the way, admiring your work as I do, I am going to ask a favour of you. May I quote some of the things you say about "Legends" in this letter? My publishers are making up a page of quotations from reviews, etc. to put in my other books, and they would very much like permission to quote some of this letter of yours there and possibly elsewhere. If you think this is cheeky of me, just say no you don't want it, but it would be a great satisfaction to me if you would let me use it. People with your insight and sympathy are rare, and your word carries weight. The reviews of "Legends" have been almost uniformly fine and complimentary, but I cannot see that many people have grasped my intention as you have done. A few have, and the papers have accorded me much space, and, after all, one does not write for the public, but for the few people whom one can really speak to. I do not know any one whom I would rather please than you. I do not think I ever write what pleases myself.

I read a few excerpts from an article of yours in an English paper on Walt Whitman.[108] It does not seem to me that you have quite got him. I doubt whether you will quite get America until you see it. It is so different from any other country, but it seems to me the only country left reasonably alive just now. We have all the vigour, and urge, and zest which all the other countries have lost, but we lack the discipline of many generations of writers behind us, therefore the English technique still beats ours. In prose, you are miles ahead of us; in poetry, I am not so sure that, taking it by and large, the American output is not better than the English just now — yours and mine excepted, of course, and watching from the side lines.

Here is another infinitesimal cheque for the half-yearly royalties on those old "Imagist Poets." You jump about so, I am a little puzzled where to address you, but I think I had better send this to the Baden Baden address as you may have left Florence before a letter can reach you.

Please give Mrs. Russell's and my love to Frieda. How I wish we could all meet again. Your mountain torrents and snow mountains fill me with envy, I who have spent the whole Summer grinding away at a belated book of Chinese translations. If it were not for my garden, which I can see out of the window, I do not know what

I should do, so much have I been confined by illness. However, I seem to be getting a little better, so I have hopes of crossing the ocean next year, but it will be only to England, I think. Will you be there?

Is your book of poems coming out? It seems to me that I saw something about it in one of the papers, but I have seen no announcement as yet.[109] I want to review it, and I want to speak for it at once if it is coming out this Autumn.

The best of luck to you both.

Affectionately yours,

Enclosures.

The account of the "Imagist Poets" is as follows:

			By sales		
Binding 50 Imagist Poets 1916		26 Imagist Poets			17.55
less folding at .105	5.25	15 "	"	1916	10.12
July 30 Balance	36.75	2 "	"	special	.51
		20 "	"	1917	13.50
	_____	1 "	"	special	.32
	42.00				42.00

1/6 of $36.75 is $6.13

66

Fontana Vecchia
Taormina
Sicilia
9 October 1921

My dear Amy

I had your letter forwarded from Baden Baden yesterday—also the cheque for six dollars. I am so sorry you have had such a summer of illness. Have you really not been able to leave your room? I call that bitter. Can you go out now? Deve finire, questo guaio.[110]

Yes, do quote anything you like from my letter, about Legends.

I said what I felt, for anybody to read or hear.

I agree with you, that American poetry today is better than English. As for me, in direction I am more than half American. I always write really towards America: my listener is there. England has gone all thick and fuzzy in the head, and can't hear. tant pis pour elle![111]

After all the shifting about, we are both so glad to be back here, in silence and peace and sunshine. It is lovely weather. The sun rises day after day red and unhidden out of the sea, after the morning star, which is very bright before he comes. I watch the dawn every day from my bed: but when the suns rim makes the first bit of fire, we get up. —I love the Ionian sea. It is open like a great blue opening in front of us, so delicate and self-contained. The hibiscus flowers are coming again in the garden. I am so thankful to come south. The north just shatters one inside. Even as far as Naples. But south of Naples—from Amalfi—there is the pristine Mediterranean influence, never to be shattered. Such a lovely *morning* world: forever morning. I hate going north—and I hate snow grinning on the tops of mountains. Jamais plus.[112]

When I gather myself together I want to set to work. I only did two poems all the summer—*Fish & Bat*. But I did "Harlequinade of the Unconscious."[113]

Have your done your Chinese book? I shall be interested to see that.

I am thankful to be at rest for the moment—but feel more than ever come loose from all moorings. I suppose I shall really leave Europe. But feel very mistrustful of the States. Wohin?[114] We shall see.

I do hope you will be better, and able to go about and taste the world. After all, one's writing is only for when there is nothing nicer to be done.

Do you have any feeling about Mexico? I have an idea I should like to go there—and have some little place in the country, with a goat and a bit of a garden. But my compass-needle is a shifty devil.

Greet Mrs Russell from us both. It must be sad for her too, if you can't go out. Be better—be on your feet, thats the chief.

Saluti cari[115]

D. H. Lawrence

67

D. H. Lawrence, Esq.
c/o Frau Baronin Von Richthofen
Ludwig-Wilhelmstift
Baden-Baden, Germany.
20 March 1922.

Dear Lawrence:

Here are our half-yearly Imagist royalties as usual, smaller than ever. It is a wonder to me they keep up. Some day these books will be out of print and then there will be no more five cent pieces coming to us on that score; but they are not quite out of print yet, and the sales dribble along as you see. The account is as follows:

By Sales

11 Imagist Poets	.67½	$7.42
7 " "	.67½	4.73
6 " "	.67½	4.05

1/6th of   16.20 is $2.70

It was awfully good of you to give me permission to use that passage from your letter. The next morning after it appeared in an advertisement, there were twenty-five copies of "Legends" ordered. Your opinion is getting to have a great deal of weight over here and I am delighted to feel that. I understand you got a prize from Edinburgh for "The Lost Girl."[116] That is good news indeed. Of course I know you will be sorry that they gave it to that book and not to one of the others, but you must not forget what the public is. And the public being what it is, I cannot help being a little sorry that you have Seltzer for a publisher. He is certainly pushing you, and that is a good thing—a very good thing—the most important thing, perhaps; but I think he has made a terrible blunder in bringing "Tortoises" out by itself. Had he brought out the whole book as I first read it in manuscript I think it would have been a splendid thing, but "Tortoises" alone seems to me a mistake. You do not want to stress your sexual side to a public incapable of understanding it. I think "Tortoises" is a very fine poem and takes its place perfectly in the whole volume as you originally planned it, but I do think it will hurt you to have it printed separately. So strongly did I feel this, that after pre-empting the book for review in the "Literary Review" of the New York "Evening Post," I gave up the idea of reviewing "Tortoises," feeling that nothing I could say about it, no matter how hard I tried, would made the public appreciate it and understand it. Mr. Seltzer is getting a name for himself as rather an erotic publisher, and that is not just the way you want your book to be taken. However, that is not my affair and you are too big to be held down inside any publisher's advertizing attitude. Seltzer tells me that he is printing that whole book of poems next year, and in order to be first on the list, I have told the "Literary Review" that I will do it whenever it comes out, for, odd though it may seem, apparently my reviews carry considerable weight.

It seems a long time since I have heard from you. Your "Sea and Sardinia" is a very fine thing, and as to the illustrator of that book — who is he? He has fairly bowled me over.[117] I am glad you are writing so much for the "Dial." I think it is the best magazine over here, and it is gaining in circulation all the time. Of course it will never equal in circulation the big pictorial monthlies, but as far as intellectual content is concerned, it is a fine magazine.

I have sent you a volume of Chinese translations which I have been doing for four years with a friend of mine who lives in China.[118] I wonder if there will be anything you will like in it. I hope so. I think these old fellows are very fine.

Meanwhile, I am pegging away at a book on Keats which I think ought to be interesting, not that he has not been written up ad nauseam, but that I think I have rather a different point of view about him, in the first place; and in the second place, that here in America there are a good many unpublished letters, etc. which the English writers have not had access to.

Also, I am mulling over a poem on my native town, its prime and decadence, which may never see the light of day, but which is a good thing to chew on in my mind in case it should ever appear.

I wonder when we shall meet. I doubt if I get to Italy for a long time. I may go to England next year, it depends upon the progress of the Keats book. I had to give up going this year in order to work at it. I do not think we are very much severed, really. Give Frieda Mrs. Russell's and my love, and keep a share for yourself.

Affectionately yours,

68

[Postcard]
Kandy.
Ceylon.
17 April. [1922]

We have been here the last six weeks—wonderful place to look at, but too hot to live in. Now we are going on to Australia—& if we don't like that, then San Francisco.—By the way I never got your last book that you said you sent me.—How are you? Write me a line c/o Robert Mountsier, 417 West 118 St. Frieda sends many greetings.

D. H. Lawrence

69

P & O. S. N. Co.
S. S.
20 May 1922

My dear Amy

Here we are rolling gently in the Great Australian Bight, on a sea swelling from the Antarctic. It is very nice. Once having started wandering I feel I shall never stop. We stayed two months in Ceylon and two weeks in West Australia. I got your letter two days ago in Perth, an hour before we sailed. Glad everything goes on.— This makes two books you have sent me to Germany, and neither of them have I got.—As for Keats, while there's a human being left on earth the last word will never be said about anything.

I am enjoying the face of the earth and letting my Muse, dear hussy, repent her ways. "Get thee to a nunnery" I said to her. Heaven knows if we shall ever see her face again, unveiled, uncoiffed.

The earth—& man—is a strange mystery: always *rather* what you expected, and yet oh, so different. So different. One wonders if all books are just so many parish magazines.—The talk is just on top.

Alas for me and my erotic reputation! Tell them I have sent my Muse into a nunnery while I took a look at the world.

I expect we shall come via the South Seas to America.

Greet Mrs Russell. Not having a secretary to sign my letter I sign it myself.

D. H. Lawrence

please address me c/o Robert Mountsier or of—Thomas Seltzer

70

Palace Hotel
San Francisco
8 Sept. 1922

Dear Amy

Well here I am under the Star-spangled Banner—though perhaps the Stripes of persecution are more appropriate.

San Francisco is sunny & pleasant, though noisy & full of the sound of iron. We leave tonight for Santa Fe. Send me a line, c/o Mrs Mabel Sterne,[119] *Taos,* New Mexico—to tell me how you are: unless of course the new prosecution of Women in Love[120] makes you feel that least said soonest mended.

We still feel a bit dazed after the long trip across the Pacific. Will take me some time in a little quiet place to myself to gather together the me that is me. Pour tous les autres, je m'en fiche.[121]

Greet Mrs Russell. Frieda sends her Wiedersehen.

D. H. Lawrence

71

12 September 1922.

Dear Lawrence:

Here is the usual bi-yearly pittance from the sales of the Imagist Anthologies. There are still a few copies left of each of the yearly issues, but I suppose they will be ended before long and then these royalties will cease altogether. I ordered them to discontinue printing them years ago, you will remember, but the sales are so slow that it takes a long time to use up the remainders they have.

By Sales:

13	Imagist Poets		.67½	8.78
4	"	" 1916	.67½	2.70
8	"	" 1917	.67½	5.40

1/6 of   16.88 is $2.82

What a globe trotter you are! Your letter from Australia gave me a perfect turn, I had no idea you were going so far afield. A very nice paper on you came out in the New York "Times" by a man whose name I forget, who saw you last year in Sicily.[122] It was most sympathetic and delightful and must tell the American public something of the real man of whom they are perfectly ignorant. It is good news to know that you are going to land on our shores before long. I hope you will, for I think now you have a public here, which I do not think you had when you thought of coming over some years ago. It is a thousand pities that "Women in Love" has been suppressed. I knew that Seltzer was going about it the best way to get it suppressed. He has not managed things cleverly, but he is a keen admirer of yours and that is a great deal. You have a really very large and appreciative public here now. I do not know anybody who has more influence or who is better liked than you.

I am awfully sorry you have lost the various books that I have sent flying after you. I suppose that they have disappeared in the mail and that you will never get them. As a matter of fact, there is only one, for you got "Legends" and the only thing that I have published since then is my Chinese Translations, which I did in collaboration with Mrs. Ayscough, "Fir-Flower Tablets." I will not send you another copy during your wanderings, but will wait until you are stationary somewhere and then send it to you.

Do let me know where you are and how you are getting on, and give a great deal of love to Frieda from Mrs. Russell and me.

Affectionately yours,

72

D. H. Lawrence, Esq.,
c/o Mrs. Mabel Sterne
Taos, New Mexico.
16 September 1922.

Dear Lawrence:

I was just going to mail this letter when yours came. A hearty welcome to these United States of America. I am delighted to know that you are here at last. Please tell me when you are thinking of coming East, for really in New Mexico you are almost as far away as in Australia.

If you think there is noise of iron in San Francisco, I wonder what you will think when you reach Chicago or New York. The country takes a good deal of getting used to, and I am a little afraid you may not like it; but there are so many different kinds of it that you ought to be able to be suited somewhere.

If you stay in Santa Fé, you will be right in the nest of my enemies, Alice Henderson and Witter Bynner[123] — how they hate me! I do not know whether Witter Bynner is still in New Mexico, but Alice Henderson lives there all the time for her health, poor child. By the way, if you search the seven seas and all the lands impinging on them, you could not find a better place for your health than New Mexico. I have not been there for thirty years, not since Indians on donkeys rode down the streets of Santa Fé arrayed in gaudily striped blankets and feathers, but they tell me that it is still lovely and very interesting. While you are there, you ought to go to some of the pueblos and see some of the ritualistic dances of the Indians, if it is not too late in the year.

If you run across my friend, Elsie Sergeant,[124] who is in Santa Fé a great part of the time, and in contradistinction to Mrs. Henderson and Mr. Bynner is one of my greatest friends, just tell her you are a friend of mine, and she will do everything to make you feel happy.

Are you really such a silly fellow as to suppose that the suppression of "Women in Love" can make a difference to me? I think "Women in Love" one of your very finest books, and this suppression business makes me sick. Everybody knows that I am one of your chief champions in this country, and, by the way, I enjoyed

"Aaron's Rod" extremely, although I do not think it as fine as "Women in Love."

I shall be very interested to hear your reactions to our country. It is so different from everything you have ever seen. Don't let its bigness and its rush "get your goat," as we say on this side of the ocean. Wait until it has had a chance to sink in a bit, and maybe you will find that there is a great internal quiet under the rush, and a restful sense of space; and as to the tyranny—well, if you are not a wine-bibber, you can get along pretty well, although I am not in favour of prohibition myself—from a purely academic standpoint, as I practically never drink anything.

Give our love, Mrs. Russell's and mine, to Frieda, and be sure you let me know when you think of turning your steps Eastward. I am thoroughly glad you are in America. It is an experience you should have, and you will understand conditions here much better when you have sojourned among us for a while. It is not as mellow as England, but lots more broad-minded and sympathetic.

Sincerely yours,

73

**Taos. New Mexico.
19 Oct. 1922**

My dear Amy

Well, we have been here for five weeks, and are more or less getting used to it. We have a gay little adobe house on the edge of the desert, with the mountains sitting round under the sun. The Indian pueblo is about two miles off, & Taos Plaza one mile. We don't see much of the "world"—save Mabel Sterne and her visitors.

The land I like exceedingly. You'd laugh to see Frieda and me trotting on these Indian ponies across the desert, and scrambling wildly up the slopes among the piñon bushes, accompanied either by an Indian, John Concha, or a Mexican, José. It is great fun. Also we go to hot springs and sit up to our necks in the clear, jumping-up water.

Of course, humanly, America does to me what I knew it would do: it just *bumps* me. I say the people charge at you like trucks coming down on you—no awareness. But one tries to dodge aside in time. Bump! bump! go the trucks. And that is human contact. One gets a sore soul, and at times yearns for the understanding mildness of Europe. Only I like the country so much.

I wasn't aware of being in a nest of your enemies: but I must have been, according to you. We slept the very first night in New Mexico at Witter Bynners house in Santa Fe, and Alice Corbin was there. They talked of you too, but everything quite nice and I should never have suspected enemies. A bit critical of your work, of course, but that goes without saying. When poets talk of my poetry I don't expect them to leave one line hanging on to another—Shreds!

Seltzer won his "case" all right, and seems mighty pleased. He sold out his *de luxe* Women in Loves and now has a two-dollar edition, I hear. He is supposed to bring out Fantasia of the Un-conscious this week. I'll send you a copy when he sends some to me: though I don't suppose it is in your line.—He urges me to come east, and has a house for me in Connecticut. But I like this land so much, and shrink from the witches cauldron of New York. So he must come to Mahomet—can't spell it—[125] for Mahomet isn't budging yet awhile.

I have done two poems here: my first in America. Wonder whom I shall send them to. Harriett Monroe has two from Birds Beasts in November's Poetry.[126]

No, the books you sent me never came on. Probably Germany wouldn't let them out without a licence. That's how it is.—I shall look forward to the new one.

You don't say how your health is: I hope it's quite mended. And I really look forward to meeting you again. So does Frieda. We both send many greetings—also to Mrs Russell.[127]

D. H. Lawrence

74

D. H. Lawrence, Esq.
Hotel Monte Carlo
Av. Uruguay 69
Mexico City
Mexico.
6 April 1923.

Dear Lawrence:

I am a bad correspondent, am I not? I must apologize very humbly on that score, but I do find it extremely difficult to keep up with my mail and my writing and my lectures all at once. I have just been making a six weeks' tour through the Middle West, during which I gave seventeen lectures in a whole galaxy of towns. Unfortunately I did not get farther West than Omaha nor farther South than Indianapolis, so I could not drop in on you at Taos, as I should have liked to have done.

I was very much interested in your article in the "Dial" about your impressions of the Indians.[128] I feel a good deal as you do on the subject. I do not want to go back to the primitive; I have not the slightest desire to lose what civilisation has gained. The picturesqueness, the colour of the Pueblo Indians, their dances, their songs—I have an immense curiosity about these, but my curiosity is entirely artistic, not in the least ethnological. I have not been in New Mexico since I was nine years old, although I remember it fairly well, strangely enough, but I have read a great deal of Indian literature since I was there. You remember "Many Swans," which you liked, and the Pueblo Indian section in it.

I gather—I do not know exactly why, because you have not said so in any of your articles—but I do gather that you are not in love with my country people. America is so vast that one section of it is very unlike another, as you will discover when you come East, and I do believe that alien nations such as the Indians and the Peons give a colour and picturesqueness to life in New Mexico and Arizona which, of course, we entirely lack on the Atlantic Coast. New York is unique, unlike anywhere in the world, I believe. Boston is much like England; mentally, extremely so. Even its scenery does not differ very greatly from English scenery. As I look out of my window where I am writing, I see my little sunken garden flanked with clipped trees on both sides, and over the greenhouse, past the shaven hedge, a road bordered by elm trees, a wide country road. I have been many times struck, in looking at just that view, with its resemblance to a garden corner, and road beyond, I once saw in Liverpool. To be sure, these elms are American elms, and the shaven hedge is maplewood rather than box or privet, and the edgings of my garden beds are of sea-thrift, not of lavender, but this place being laid out shortly after the Revolution, it was done "in the English taste," as the old garden books say. My house is definitely Georgian red brick. My library is panelled with English oak; so, when you come to see me, you will probably find yourself in the uninteresting surroundings of complete familiarity.

Seltzer tells me that you have gone to old Mexico. I have never been there, it must be exceedingly picturesque. But I see through your adventuring so far that you are trying to get away from that crude and importunate America with which you feel little sympathy, you are searching [for] something with deeper roots and a more conscious background. I bet that is it, and I want to know if I am right.

You do not seem to have written to me as much as usual either, although I believe it is you who wrote the last letter. But do not confuse me with the "juggernaut trucks" you spoke of. I wonder if you remember that, in your first letter on American soil, you likened my country people to those machines. When are you coming East? The Summer is the best time for that, and you should go up to New Hampshire and Maine and see the old New England country, which is really very beautiful. And you and Frieda should make us a visit on the way.

Here, by the way, is the pittance of our half-yearly royalties on those "Imagist Anthologies." They should have been sent to you in February, but in February I was rushing from town to town and could not attend to anything of the kind, and as the cheque is so idiotically small I did not suppose it mattered. You will see by the amount of copies still on hand that the books will be out of print before very long. As I do not know where you are, nor where you will be when this letter reaches you, nor your address (on second thoughts I will wire to Seltzer and ask him that), I am in two minds as to whether to send you my cheque for the money or a money order. My cheque would be of no use to you in Mexico, I imagine, and I cannot make out a money order until I know whether it is to be a Mexican money order or not. You can cash my personal cheque anywhere in America. I will ask Seltzer how long you intend to stay in Mexico and post this letter on hearing from him.

114

Mrs. Russell joins me in sending a great deal of love to both you and Frieda. I am longing to see you both. After all, do not forget that, although I am not doing any reviewing now, I was the first person to write about you in this country so far as I know, which I consider a most happy distinction for me.

With a great deal of love,

Affectionately yours,

Statement of Account.

By sales to Jan. 31, 1923:

21 Imagists Poets	at .67½	$14.18	
13 " 1916	at .67½	8.77	
13 " 1917	at .67½	8.78	
	1/6 of	$31.73	is $5.29.

On hand Jan. 31, Imagists Poets, 25; Imagists 1916, 23; Imagists 1917, 31.

75

Hotel Monte Carlo. Av. Uruguay 69. Mexico D. F.
21 April 1923

Dear Amy

I have your letter, & the *ciro postale*. Here we are, circling uneasily round, wondering whether we shall settle for a time, or not. I would like to sit down and write a novel on the American continent (I don't mean *about* it: I mean while I'm here). But it is hard to break through the wall of the atmosphere.—I didn't really dislike the U. S. A. as much as I expected. And I don't *mistrust* it half as much as I mistrust the present England, with its false sentimentalism. So I hesitate here.

Probably I shall come to New York, by sea, before the autumn passes. Then we should both very much like to pay you a little visit, if you feel equal to visitors. While the flowers still last in your garden.

Mexico *is* interesting—but I feel I haven't got the right hang of it yet.

Remember us to Mrs Russell — and I do hope you are feeling well & strong.

Yrs ever

D. H. Lawrence

76

**Telephone: RIverside 4354
care Seltzer. 5 W. 50th St
New York
3 July 1923**

Dear Amy

We came in to town yesterday, & have your letter.

We neither of us want to go without seeing you. We should like to come for a couple of days. Probably we sail the 18th. — I am not sure. I balk going.

Write and tell me when we shall come — only not the next week-end — 11th & 12th. And tell me a train from New York, will you: preferably after 10 a. m. Because we are really staying in a Seltzer cottage in New Jersey, & have to come in to town. Perhaps best write to the cottage — as Mr Seltzer doesn't always come out with the letters.

Mr Hammerslaugh's Cottage
  Union Hill
    Dover. New Jersey
Greet Mrs Russell from us both.
Shall be glad to see you.

D. H. Lawrence

116

77

care Thomas Seltzer. 5. West 50th St. *New York City*
23 July 1923

Dear Amy

Here we are — in the Seltzer's Cottage in New Jersey at the moment. Probably you are a thousand miles away. But let me know: & tell me if there is to be a meeting. I think we sail for England about 20th August.
Greetings to you.

D. H. Lawrence

78

D. H. Lawrence, Esq.
c/o Thomas Seltzer Publisher
5 West 50th St.
New York City.
1 August 1923.

Dear Lawrence:

Of course I want you and Frieda to come and give me a few days before you go back to England. I should be heartbroken if I did not see you at all, and I want you to see this old place on which I was born; although it is not anything especial, I am very fond of it. I do wish you had come earlier when we had lots of room, Mrs. Russell and I being alone. Now, however, and for the rest of the Summer, Mrs. Russell's daughter and her family are with us, but if you and Frieda do not mind inconvenient rooms on the top floor, you will find them at least full of welcome.

I warn you that there never was a deader place than this is in Summer, everyone flits to some Summer place. However, if you do not mind sitting round and looking at the garden and talking to Mrs. Russell and me, I think you will find a few days here pleasant enough. Certainly we have a lot to say as we have not met for so long.

You say you sail on the twentieth of August. Is that definite,

117

or merely an approximate date? You say "about." I suppose you will sail from New York, most people do. However, there is plenty of time to come over before that. I have no engagements except with Mr. John Keats, with whom I am spending most of my time at present, and the book is slowly marching forward, but both he and I will accommodate ourselves to your engagements.

Mrs. Russell and I both send our love to Frieda.

Very sincerely yours,

79

care Seltzer. 5 West 50th St.
New York.
7 August 1923

Dear Amy

This to say perhaps you had better write to the New York address, as it is not very certain if the post will find us here in New Jersey.

I doubt if I shall get myself as far as England. Feel I dont want to go. But Frieda will sail on the 18th—and I shall sail somewhere or other.

Au revoir

D. H. Lawrence

80

D. H. Lawrence, Esq.
Mr. Hammerslaugh's Cottage
Union Hill Dover N.J.
7 August 1923.

Dear Lawrence:

It is too bad you cannot come over next Sunday, that would be a good time. However, suppose you come over for the Sunday after, if you decide not to sail for England on the eighteenth. If you decide to go to England on the eighteenth, why not come over on Tuesday and stay until Friday, when I suppose you must go back to catch your steamer.

The trains from New York are legion, they go, I think, practically every hour. I think the best one to take is the one o'clock limited, which would get you here at six, comfortably in time for dinner. Do not go straight through to the South Station—get out at the stop before, which is called Back Bay Station, and there my motor will meet you and bring whatever hand luggage you have with you. If you have any trunks, please let me know, and I will send an express wagon for them. I suppose, however, you will probably leave your heavy luggage behind in New York, as you undoubtedly sail from there. If you should have any luggage to check, check it at the Back Bay Station.

We shall be awfully glad to see you and Frieda again. You must not expect excitement, this place is as quiet as the grave, but then I think I told you that before.

Love to Frieda from us both.

Very sincerely yours,

81

New Jersey.
Friday
[10 August 1923]

Dear Amy

I had already gone to sleep when you telephoned.

Frieda leaves next Saturday, & I the next week. She of course put off dentist till the last few days. So I don't see how we can come. Which is disappointing.—This was our free week. The next is a thousand and one things to do.

But we shall probably be in New York again soon.—Then we'll see you, surely.—I am sorry about this time.

Greet Mrs Russell.

Yours ever.

D. H. Lawrence

82

D. H. Lawrence Esq.
Mr. Hammerslaugh's Cottage
R.F.D. No. 1
Dover, New Jersey
15 August 1923

Dear Lawrence:

I am more disappointed than I can say that you and Frieda cannot come on, I had looked forward so much to seeing you. It was a catenation of circumstances which prevented our meeting this week.

You have no idea how slow the mails are in this part of the world. I did not receive your letter telling me when you were to sail until a week ago yesterday, and there was not time then to get you over here and back before Sunday when you said you were engaged; therefore, the best I could do was to ask you for this week. I wish I could have extended my invitation to you beyond the date when Frieda had to leave, but the truth of the matter is that I am not very strong, and it requires all the strength I have to keep up my work and do practically nothing else. Therefore, I can never have people stay in the house for more than two or three days at a time. I have not been able to for some years; I enjoy them too much and get all tired out. But I had looked forward tremendously to having some long talks with you and picking up threads which time and distance have made it impossible to keep in hand. Do not forget that I am your earliest, if not your sincerest, friend in this country. Your success has given me the greatest pleasure. I do very little reviewing now, and I do not review fiction, or you would have seen my name attached to many admiring reviews as in the past.

What I particularly wanted to know was whether you were going to give us another volume of poetry before long; in fact, there were so many things I wanted to know that now I feel as if I had been suddenly corked up, and the sensation is very unpleasant.

Both Mrs. Russell and I remember Frieda with so much affection that we were very anxious to see her too. As I wrote her a couple of days ago, I fear that you do not like the country well enough to come again soon as you suggest.[129] I think I could have given you a much pleasanter impression of it than any you have had, but perhaps that is conceited of me. At any rate, there are several

120

people here who will be very disappointed when I tell them that they are not going to see you after all.

Do write me a nice long letter and tell me something about yourself and your state of mind. In the gossiping world of poetry I hear so many different accounts of your point of view that I am trying to reconcile what I hear with what I knew, and don't you dare to come as near me as New York again and not come over. Let me know where you go and what your address will be.

I am enclosing the usual pittance for the Imagist royalties. At this rate I think in two or three years they will cease altogether, and I shall be very glad when they do. They are not enough to amount to anything and distributing them twice a year is a bore. As almost all the poems in them are printed in our books, I cannot see why people go on buying them at all; however, they do.

With best wishes for Frieda's journey to England and yours to wherever it may be,

Affectionately yours,

By sales:

19 Imagist Poets			.67½	12.82
12	"	" 1916	"	8.10
13	"	" 1917	"	8.77
		1/6 of		$ 29.69 is $4.95

83

N. Jersey. Saturday evening
18 Aug [1923]

My dear Amy

I have just got back from seeing Frieda off on the steamer, & found your letter. — I'm sorry we are not seeing you. I wasn't very sure if you wanted to be troubled by visitors. I knew of course your health was not good.

But I have always a very warm memory of you in those days in England: the Berkeley, & when you came with Mrs Russell to that cottage. — Tempi passati! Già troppo passato![130]

I ought to have gone to England. I wanted to go. But my inside self wouldn't let me. At the moment I just can't face my own country again. It makes me feel unhappy, like a terrible load.

But I don't care for New York. I feel the people one sees want to jeer at us. They come with a sort of pre-determination to jeer. — But that is literary.

I am going West again — to Los Angeles, & then, if I can get a sailing ship of some sort, out to sea. This New York leaves me with one great desire, to get away from people altogether. That is why I can't go to Europe: because of the many people, the many things I shall have to say, when my soul is mute towards almost everybody.

Seltzer is bringing out various books of mine, & I have asked him to send you a copy of each. — The poems, *Birds Beasts & Flowers,* should be done — published I mean — by Sept 20th. I'll ask Seltzer to send you an advance copy. But don't review it unless you *really* feel like it.

Thank you for the little cheque. Sending these tiny sums is a nuisance to you; don't bother to do it, give the money to somebody who is poor.

Frieda wanted to see England again: it is four years since we were there. And her mother in Baden Baden. My heart goes like lead when I think of England or Germany. — I am thankful we are no longer poor, so that we can take our way across the world.

Either Frieda will come and join me somewhere west — perhaps in Mexico: or I shall go to her in Europe. In which latter case, I'll let you know in plenty of time. And then tell me if you really want me to come: if you feel equal to the effort of visitors. As for me, I never want to be a visitor for longer than two days. That is enough.

But we'll keep a bit of decent kindliness at the bottom of our hearts, as we had ten years ago. I'll never let the world bankrupt me *quite* in this.

Greet Mrs Russell. I hope you'll feel strong again.

D. H. Lawrence

I am leaving this Cottage for good on Monday — expect to leave New York on Tuesday.

D. H. L.

122

84

D. H. Lawrence, Esq.
care of Thomas Seltzer, Inc.
5 West Fiftieth St.
New York City.
31 December 1924.

Dear Lawrence:

I hear you are still at Taos, but, as I do not know for certain, I am going to send this letter care of Thomas Seltzer. I wish I could have reviewed your last book of poems, but I was absolutely drowned in my life of Keats and could do nothing outside; I knew you would understand.

Our little Imagist anthologies are gradually giving up the ghost. I am sending you enclosed a cheque for the February and August statements. They were both so small that I thought it better to keep them and send them together. Here is the account:

3 Imagist Poets		at	.67½	2.03	
10 "	"	1916 at	.67½	6.75	
11 "	"	1917 at	"	7.43	
		1/6 of		16.21 is $2.70	

The first two anthologies went out of print with the August statement, and there are only six copies of the "1917" left, so we shall soon have done with them altogether, and these remittances of two cents a time will disappear.

Someone told me that Frieda had come back and was with you now in New Mexico. I wish we might have met last year, and I hope we shall have a chance of meeting again before long.

Mrs. Russell and I are sailing for England in April, I am to give some lectures and talks there, and we expect to stay about three months, when we shall return to these diggins and settle down as usual. I expect to have another book of poems out a year from now. I have not read your last book, "The Boy in the Bush," because I have read nothing since I have been working on the Keats. Some day I hope to be able to read again; just now I am too tired to do anything but sleep and eat, for Keats was an awful task and I am thankful that it is over.

You are the most indefatigable worker I ever saw; your energy amazes me. My many operations took a great deal of my energy away, but I hope to get it back again some day. I hear rumours that you hated New York, at which I am not in the least surprised, and that you like New Mexico, which does not surprise me either, but I wish you could come on here because I think you might like this place, although not as much as New Mexico I imagine.

I hear from Hilda occasionally and from Richard once in a while, and I hope to pick up the threads of many things when I return to England. I am only sorry that you and Frieda are not going to be there. I would send you the Keats when it comes out, but I doubt very much whether you will care for it; however, you shall have it if the idea seems in the least attractive to you, but beware, it is in two large volumes!

I read your book on American literature with a great deal of interest, and not a little divergence of view. The Puritans were not so puritanical as they have been represented, but it takes some time to know that. Neither is any corner of America America; until you have seen the whole of it you cannot be said to have seen it at all. But of course, you dear prejudiced soul, you will never believe that. If you will come to me without fail the next time you are in this region, I can show you something you have not yet seen.

Give my love to Frieda, in which Mrs. Russell joins, and love to you from both of us also.

Affectionately yours,

85

Av. Pino Suarez #43. *Oaxaca* (Oax) Mexico 16 Jan 1925.

Dear Amy

Thank you for your letter & the little cheque.

We were the summer in New Mexico—you know Frieda is now the proud possessor of a little ranch there, up in the mountains, about 17 miles from Taos. But we came down here end of October, because of the cold. It got my chest a bit: or the altitude: 8,500 ft. I expect we shall go back there in the summer: like it very much: Come & see us one day.

But about March I think we shall go to England & Germany,

for a month or two. Frieda's mother is very old, & keeps wanting her to go home. And my father died, & my sisters keep wanting to see me.—Probably we shall be in London when you are. If so, I hope to see you again: it was 1914, & Richard was not yet a soldier—You can always find me c/o Curtis Brown

6 Henrietta St

Covent Garden.

W. C. 2

He's in the telephone book: is a literary agent.

I should like very much to have Keats. Am as a matter of fact rather fond of fat two-vol books with letters in them and all that.

Did my Quetzalcoatl novel down here.[131] It scares me a bit. But it's nearly done.

I wonder where I should ask you to send me the Keats book. Perhaps best c/o Curtis Brown and *to await arrival.* Tell them to mark it that, please. Then perhaps I'll review it in London. A threat!—But I should like to have it.—And if you tell either Thomas Seltzer or Martin Secker to give you the Boy in the Bush from me, they'll do it at once.

It's awful to have such a bad time with your health.

I never said I knew all America: or all about it. God forbid! and keep on forbidding!

One day, perhaps, we may be aimiable to one another for half an hour in your Brooklyn Garden. If pansies are out—Jusqu' a-lors![132]—or no, till London again.[133]

Yrs

D. H. Lawrence

Frieda sends saluti e ricordi.[134]
Remember us to Mrs Russell.

D. H. L.

86

Del Monte Ranch.
Questa
New Mexico
6 April 1925

Dear Amy

I have so often wondered if you are sitting in London, in the Berkeley, maybe: & see where we are. I got malaria in Oaxaca: then grippe: then a typhoid inside: was so sick, I wearied of the day. Struggled to Mexico, was put to bed again for three weeks — then packed off up here. We had booked our passages to England, but the doctor said I *must* stay in the sun, he wouldn't be answerable for me if I went on the sea, & to England. So we came here. The Emigration Authorites at El Paso treated us as Emigrants, & nearly killed me a second time: this after the consul & the Embassy people in Mexico — the Americans — had been most kind, doing things to make it easier for us. They only made it harder. The Emigration Dept is Dept of Labour, & you taste the Bolshevist method at its crudest.

However — after two days fight we got through — & yesterday got to our little ranch. There is snow behind the house, & sky threatening snow. But usually it's brilliantly sunny. And the log fire is warm. And the Indian Trinidad is chopping wood under the pine tree, & his wife Lufina, in her wide white boots, is shuffling carrying water. I begin to feel better: though still feel I don't care whether it's day or night.

I saw notices of your Keats book. Pity after all I didn't ask you to send the promised copy here: I could have wandered in it now. But I'll write to Curtis Brown. And I'll send you a copy of my little novel *St Mawr*.

I managed to finish my Mexican novel *Quetzalcoatl* in Mexico: the very day I went down, as if shot in the intestines. But I daren't even look at the outside of the MS. It cost one so much: & I wish I could eat all the lotus that ever budded, & drink up Lethe to the source. Talk about dull opiates — one wants something that'll go into the very soul.

Send a line to say where you are and how you are liking it. If you come west, come and see us. I hope to get to Europe in the autumn. Frieda is happy arranging her house.

Souvenirs!

D. H. Lawrence

87

D. H. Lawrence, Esq.
Del Monte Ranch
Questa, New Mexico
22 April 1925.

My dear Mr. Lawrence:

You will be sorry to hear that Miss Lowell too is very ill, and has been obliged to give up the lecture trip to England which she had planned to take this Spring. The doctors would not allow her to take the ocean voyage at this time with the possibility of an emergency operation on the steamer where the facilities are so limited. They are keeping her very quiet now in the hope of avoiding an operation which she is in no condition to undergo after the long work on "John Keats." She is bitterly disappointed as you can imagine, for this was the moment of all others for her to go to England.[135]

Yours very truly,

Secretary.

LETTERS BETWEEN FRIEDA LAWRENCE AND AMY LOWELL

88

[ca. 16 October 1914]

Dear Miss Lowell,

How awfully nice it is of you, how you have the "art of giving"! That typewriter is something to live for—I think we must have been feeling kindly towards each other because I remembered that you liked manuscripts and wondered if you would like any more of L.'s stuff—perhaps you prefer poetry to prose—Your picture of your friends coming sounds delightful, how are the dogs that Mrs Russel was suffering from? We had two of the same family here, the Cannans. You are truly an angel to do that nasty job the Mitchell Kennerley job, I mean—A friend told us they had read a review of your poems, (they will send it.) It said, they were beautiful, praised them, but the *language* they did not approve off—It's the same old cry, if you go your own way, they would like to bring you back to the old well worn path of ages—Critics really are not clever, in understanding *new* things—Only *established* people—I hope it has given you satisfaction, the book, I shall look forward to it!

Good-bye and many, many thanks.

yours very sincerely

Frieda Lawrence

89

My dear Miss Lowell,

I am so worried about Lawrence's health—when these wet, dark wintermonth come, it's a perpetual anxiety—I know Italy would be so much better for him—he felt so much better there—Last winter practically did for him here in England—We are very badly off, but you know once we are in Italy we can live very cheaply there. Compton Mackenzie has offered us a house—I know how really generous you are and I ask you to help us a little—It would be so infinitely welcome just at the moment. I saw Pinker the agent who has every confidence that L's work will pay *some* day, but at present the wolf seems to find our doorstep a very comfortable place—Do help us, dear Miss Lowell, if you possibly can—With kindest regards hoping to have some jolly times with you again before very long.

Yours affectionately

Frieda Lawrence

90

Dear Amy Lowell,

I never pass the Berkeley hotel without thinking of you there and the jolly evening we had. Alas, times seem very much sadder now, the world in such a stew everywhere; where and when will it be the end or any end or any beginning? We are out of the raids here anyhow, did you hear that H. D.'s rooms were bombed people take it so coolly, but when they come night after night then it's most nerveshattering. It's a different London than the London you knew. We are very poor at present, even for us low watermark, mostly I dont mind but just occasionally when Lawr is seedy and I get scared, that's why I cant tell you, how glad it makes me that Hilda A. said you would help us again! I am very grateful. It is a load of me at present and one has quite enough to burden one as it is—It is generous of you! Hilda gets very low at times, it is'nt good for her to be alone and Richard away, she feels it very much— We had some very jolly evenings with them, but though we enjoyed it, there was always underneath something sad but we acted all sorts of mad things and wished you were there! One thing we saw was really beautiful: Russian Opera, very wonderful music. Lawrence is writing another novel[136]—There is a rather charming young poet Robert Nicholls, (he was Oxford and wounded in France,) in America now, I think you would like him! Hoping to see you before long when we shall be very gay.

With best wishes for your health—I saw a paper with photographs of your beautiful house—Lawrence wishes to send his kindest respects—

Yours very sincerely

Frieda Lawrence

91

Chapel Farm Cottage
Hermitage
nr Newbury
Berks
April 15th. [1918]

Dear Amy Lowell,

Thank you very much for your gift—It was most specially welcome in these hard times. Lawrence is in the Midlands, so I send you these few words about him quickly, as he is a duffer at saying anything about himself—This war is dreadful and this last battle the most dreadful part of it—It makes one quite numb and stupid—Poor humanity, poor world! But you are fine working as your are doing! I am sure he did not get your letter asking him for a biography, so dont be cross with him. Hilda is in Cornwall which is very lovely in the spring—This also is very charming, the Thomas Hardy country you know. Lawrence will write to you so I will send this off quickly!

With all the best wishes in the world and many, many thanks.

Yours

Frieda Lawrence

I hope, what I said will be a little use to you!

To understand D. H. Lawrence one must know that he belongs to the Midlands, to that navel of England, the country of George Elliot and more or less the country of the Brontés and Mrs Gaskell. It is a strange black country with an underworld quality that is rather frightening. In Sons and Lovers the life of the miner, the life of the common people has perhaps for the first time been written from the *inside,* not from the point of the intellectual, not with pity as a Galsworthy presents it, but showing for the first time the richness of this class, a living from realities, it is another centre from which they live—The intellectual or educated can hardly conceive this form of life; by their very education they have sacrificed it. And in D. H. L. it has become articulate for the first time. At the present moment the world is despairing for this lost reality and trying to regain this Paradise lost. Sons and Lovers is more or less a biography. One may admire or not admire D. H. L.'s art, but the absolute genuineness and freshness of it nobody can deny; there is no secondhand of feeling or thinking, it is all fresh and new as a larch tree in spring. D. H. L. was born in Eastwood nr Nottingham in 1884,[137] went to school at Nottingham and then to University College there. It is rather remarkable that he distinguished himself in several subjects but in English composition he was found unsatisfactory![138] Then he taught at Croydon. His mode of teaching must have been rather unconventional, but none the less effective. In English history for instance he did not only expound the battle of Agincourt, but arranged the boys in two sides and they *fought* the battle of Agincourt over schoolforms and all. Then came the great and deep first shock of his mother's death.

This undermined his health he gave up teaching and devoted himself entirely to writing. In 1914 he married and has since lived a very simple life partly in Italy and lastly in Cornwall. This celtic country cast a spell over him with its unsolved mysteries. Looking across the Atlantic from his small Cornish Cottage he sometimes longed to be another Columbus and discover America for himself, he has a great faith in the America of the future. American Litterature has his profound admiration. Its true significance, he thinks, has never been thoroughly understood either here in Europe or America itself. He is at present writing a book on "the mystic significance of American Classic Litterature."

92

Mrs. D. H. Lawrence,
Chapel Farm Cottage,
Hermitage nr. Newbury,
Berks, England.
13 August 1919.

Dear Frieda:

I am terribly afraid that Lawrence will misunderstand or be dreadfully hurt at the letter I have just been obliged to write him.

I do not think that he realizes the difficulty of getting on over here and the terrible expense of living. It is almost impossible for any one trained in the older methods to write acceptably for the papers here, and Lawrence has never been a journalist, and there is nothing else that offers anything like a sure income. I do not know any papers here which would welcome his work as a steady contributor. He knows England and knows it well, but neither English subjects nor English authors are very welcome here to-day, except for those few novelists that the public has adopted. I fear for him nothing but bitter disappointment and despair if he attempts to come over without having some definite plan arranged. I would take him under my roof in a moment, but that my own health is precarious and I dare not have guests, as I find that no matter how much I like them, they try me too much; and I am in no position to guarantee him any income until he is able to earn it for himself. If Mr. Huebsch can get him anything definite before he comes, that would put an entirely different complexion on the matter, and he might be able to succeed, but America is no more radical than England; in some ways it is less so, and I do not think that he will find that there is any field for his work here. I hate to have to say this; I hate to have to think it, but this is not the country I am sure. Of course, if he comes, I will do everything for him that I can, and naturally I should not let him get stuck, but I do not want him to feel that I am a possible resort, as I do not think I ought to take on any such attitude, and I think that he should have some definite idea as to what he can do before he comes here.

Please try to make him understand that I only write this to help him and that if he decides after all to come, everything which my influence can do and that my friendship could dictate shall be done for his benefit.

Always sincerely yours,

93

Tuesday
Morris plains
Union Hill
[14 August 1923]

Dear Amy,

You wrote me a very nice letter and thank you very much—No, I did want to come and I wanted to see you—I have not forgotten how you befriended us when we were nobodies! Is it really nine years ago? We cant come now, I have a dentist to go to and I hope you will not be cross—But I am coming back from Europe before very long and may I write to you and come then? Lawrence cant make up his mind to go to Europe, he just cant, so I am going alone—I am very glad you are well, I just heard your voice saying that, but no more, I am an idiot with a telefone—So I hope to see you before long.

With all very good wishes and many thanks.

Yours

Frieda Lawrence

NOTES

[1] Amy Lowell met Richard Aldington and his American wife Hilda Doolittle (H.D.) because they were prominent Imagists who had appeared in Pound's *Des Imagistes*. Along with John Gould Fletcher, they were guests at the Berkeley Hotel dinner on 30 July 1914 at which the Lawrences first met Lowell. Aldington, H.D., and Fletcher would be featured with Lawrence in Lowell's three annuals, *Some Imagist Poets*. (The sixth poet included in the anthologies was F. S. Flint.)

[2] Lowell first met the actress Ada Dwyer Russell in March 1912. When illness forced Russell to leave the stage, Lowell offered her the position of "companion" at a salary equal to what she had earned as an actress. Russell served in that capacity from May 1914 until Lowell's death in May 1925. Lawrence's greetings to Mrs. Russell are an almost ritual feature of his letters to Lowell.

[3] Lawrence regularly misspells the first name of Harriet Monroe, the longtime editor of *Poetry*.

[4] The Lawrence poems actually published in the 1915 edition of *Some Imagist Poets* are "Ballad of Another Ophelia," "Illicit," "Fireflies in the Corn," "A Woman and Her Dead Husband," "The Mowers," "Scent of Irises," and "Green."

[5] The bad check was for Kennerley's American edition of *Sons and Lovers*. The date of the check was altered, and Lawrence's bank in Spezia wouldn't accept it. Lowell followed up on Lawrence's request, but Kennerley never made good on the check.

[6] Lowell was devoted to the seven pedigreed English sheep dogs she kept at Sevenels, her home in Brookline, Massachusetts. Lowell was assembling the poems for *Some Imagist Poets*, to be published in April 1915.

[7] "Do you know the land where the lemons bloom?" (Goethe, *Wilhelm Meister*, Book III, Chapter I.)

[8] J. B. Pinker was Lawrence's literary agent from July 1914 until December 1919.

[9] *The Rainbow*, which Kennerley did not publish.

[10] "Oh dear—oh dear!"

[11] "The golden oranges glow in the darkening foliage." (Goethe, *Wilhelm Meister*, Book III, Chapter I.)

[12] Wanting to help Lawrence without offending him, Lowell had sent him a typewriter she was discarding. Lawrence made some use of this machine in completing *The Rainbow*, and in 1916 he typed about two-thirds of *Women in Love* on it.

[13] "Knock on wood."

[14] The Royal Literary Fund gave financial assistance to deserving needy writers.

[15] *Sword Blades and Poppy Seed* (1914).

[16] Lowell was trying to interest her own publisher, Houghton Mifflin, in bringing out the first American edition of *The Prussian Officer and Other Stories*. Instead B. W. Huebsch published the collection in America in 1916.

[17] "Many cordial greetings, highly esteemed madam."

[18] Lawrence refers to a passage in Lowell's prose-poem "The Bombardment." The day before he had complained to Harriet Monroe, ". . . how dare Amy talk about bohemian glass and stalks of flame?" (*The Letters of D. H. Lawrence*, Volume II, ed. George J. Zytaruk and James T. Boulton, Cambridge University Press, 1981, p. 232).

[19] In the preface to *Sword Blades and Poppy Seed* Lowell professes a debt to French poetry.

[20] The "long poem" is "Sword Blades and Poppy Seed," and the "one about the dog" is "Fool's Money Bags." "A Taxi" is actually "The Taxi."

[21] Lawrence is referring to "A Tulip Garden."

[22] Lawrence had been asked to do a small book on Hardy by James Nisbet and Co. The "Study of Thomas Hardy" was not published until 1936 in *Phoenix*.

[23] The letters from Lowell to Lawrence were mostly sent from Sevenels in Brookline.

[24] Lowell's friend, a director of Houghton Mifflin. In 1946 Greenslet published *The Lowells and Their Seven Worlds*.

[25] The lectures, delivered in Boston in February and March 1915, were published as *Six French Poets: Studies in Contemporary Poetry* (1915).

[26] *The Prussian Officer and Other Stories*.

[27] Lawrence refers to Richard Jefferies' *The Story of My Heart* (1883), a work he found too emotionally revealing.

[28] Lawrence's good friend S. S. Koteliansky ("Kot").

[29] Frieda's yearning to see her children was a source of tension between her and Lawrence.

[30] *Some Imagist Poets: An Anthology* (1915).

[31] *The Rainbow* and *Twilight in Italy*.

[32] *The Signature* was a collaboration of Lawrence, John Middleton Murry, and Murry's wife Katherine Mansfield. It lasted only three numbers.

[33] *Six French Poets.*

[34] *The Prussian Officer and Other Stories.*

[35] In November 1915 a court order was issued for *The Rainbow* "to be destroyed at the expiration of seven days." The attempts to protest this ruling were scattered and ineffective.

[36] This moral crusader was the longtime secretary and special agent for the New York Society for the Suppression of Vice. He was instrumental in getting the law passed in 1873 that closed the mails to "obscene and indecent matter." He was famous for his raids against people he considered dealers in obscene literature. He died in September 1915.

[37] *Georgian Poetry 1913-1915*, issued in November 1915, was the most commercially successful of the five anthologies of Georgian poetry published between 1912 and 1922 by the Poetry Bookshop. Lawrence's "Service of All the Dead" and "Meeting Among the Mountains" are in the 1913-15 volume.

[38] Edgar Lee Masters' *Spoon River Anthology,* published in 1915, had taken the poetic world by storm. Émile Verhaeren was the foremost Belgian poet who wrote in French. He died in 1916. Lowell devotes a chapter to him in *Six French Poets.*

[39] *Some Imagist Poets, 1916* contains Lawrence's "Erinnyes," "Perfidy," "At the Window," "In Trouble and Shame," and "Brooding Grief."

[40] No letter from Lawrence to Lowell dated 10 January 1916 has survived.

[41] Lowell is referring to the six-point Imagist credo included in the preface.

[42] The five poems listed by Lowell are the Lawrence poems that appear in the 1916 volume of *Some Imagist Poets.* "At a Window" is "At the Window," "For Trouble and Shame" is "In Trouble and Shame."

[43] *Men, Women and Ghosts* was published in October 1916.

[44] The contract for these two books was transferred to B. W. Huebsch, which published both of them in 1916.

[45] "Give me some peace down there, damn it!"

[46] Mary Aldis's review is entitled "Some Imagist Poets" (*Little Review,* Volume 3, Number 4, June-July 1916, pp. 26-31). She especially admires Lowell's "Patterns" and Lawrence's "Erinnyes." William Lyon Phelps comments favorably on the 1916 *Some Imagist Poets* in the *Poetry Review of America* for July 1916 (Volume 1, Number 3, pp. 43-44).

[47] Lowell called her sixty-acre property in Dublin, New Hampshire, "Broomley Lacey."

⁴⁸ Monroe jointly reviewed the 1916 *Some Imagist Poets* and *Georgian Poetry: 1913-1915* in the August 1916 number of *Poetry* (Volume 8, Number 5, pp. 255-9). She writes that "no one has felt each bitter wound of this war more cruelly than [Lawrence], no one has touched the subject with more tragic beauty than he in Erinnyes" (pp. 258-59).

⁴⁹ *Twilight in Italy.*

⁵⁰ Bloodbrotherhood.

⁵¹ Ultimately this phrase found its way into Lawrence's title, *Studies in Classic American Literature*. He began writing the book in August 1917. *Studies* contains chapters on *Letters from an American Farmer, Moby Dick*, and *Two Years Before the Mast.*

⁵² Frieda had written Lowell in October 1916. Cf. Letter 88.

⁵³ "Hammers" is actually "The Hammers." The first section (or movement) of this poem, "Frindsbury, Kent, 1786," is about the building and launching of the *Bellerophon;* Lawrence refers to this section as the "Ship." "Hoops" is the first section of "A Roxbury Garden." "An Opera House" and "An Aquarium" are two sections of "Towns in Colour."

⁵⁴ "Bath" is the first section of the prose-poem "Spring Day." Lawrence also refers to "The Red Lacquer Music-Stand," "An Aquarium" (the fifth section of "Towns in Colour"), "Stravinsky's Three Pieces 'Grotesques,' for String Quartet," and "A Roxbury Garden." Lawrence's discussion of Lowell's poetry in terms of the "physico-sensational world" and "things non-human" interestingly recalls the famous letter he had written Edward Garnett about *The Rainbow* on 5 June 1914. Both letters also invoke Italian Futurism.

⁵⁵ The quotations, in which Lawrence ignores Lowell's punctuation, are from "An Aquarium" and "An Opera House."

⁵⁶A month later Lawrence wrote A. W. McLeod that Amy Lowell "is not a good poetess, I think" (*The Letters of D. H. Lawrence,* Volume III, ed. James T. Boulton and Andrew Robertson, Cambridge University Press, 1984, p. 61).

⁵⁷ Percival Lawrence, the astronomer, died suddenly after a stroke on 13 November 1916.

⁵⁸ This famous saying can be traced back to an ancient Greek fragment. In Boswell's *Life of Johnson* the phrase is quoted as a saying which everyone knows but which no one knows where to find.

⁵⁹ "The Reality of Peace" appeared in the May, June, and July 1917 issues of the *English Review.*

⁶⁰ "The Thimble" appeared in the March 1917 issue of *The Seven Arts,* "The Mortal Coil" in the July 1917 issue. The magazine merged with the *Dial* in October 1917.

[61] "Guns as Keys."

[62] "Nothing of him that doth fade / But doth suffer a sea-change / Into something rich and strange." (*The Tempest*, Act I, Scene 2.)

[63] "That's impossible!"

[64] The *Times Literary Supplement* review of *Look! We Have Come Through!* appeared on 22 November 1917, p. 571. The reviewer complains about "verbiage" and "orgies of extreme eroticism."

[65] Fletcher, recalling this meeting, said that "Lawrence interested me almost equally with his fierce, feverish intensity of spirit combined with marked physical frailty, and with his bitter and outspoken hatred of his own country." Fletcher was "moved by the passionate intensity with which Lawrence proclaimed these sentiments, no less than by the grain of appalling truth that lay underneath them" (Fletcher, *Life Is My Song*, New York, 1937, p. 244).

[66] Lowell's two lectures on "Imagism Past and Present" were delivered at the Brooklyn Institute on 20 and 27 March 1918.

[67] Lawrence considered both *Coming Awake* and *Chorus of Women* as titles for the book of poems ultimately published as *New Poems* in October 1918. "Apprehension" is the first poem of the collection.

[68] Frieda's rather eccentric biographical sketch of Lawrence is included in the letter Frieda wrote Lowell on 15 April 1918, Letter 91.

[69] *Can Grande's Castle*, published in September 1918.

[70] Nichols (1893-1944), who had a certain currency as a war poet, first met Lawrence in 1915. *Ardours and Endurances* was published in 1917. In February 1919 Nichols was the replacement for Lowell and Alfred Noyes at a Philadelphia reading when both were suffering from influenza-related illnesses. Oddly, Nichols was one of the persons at Lawrence's burial on 4 March 1930.

[71] This review, entitled "A Modern Evangelist," appeared in the August 1918 number of *Poetry* (Volume 12, Number 5, pp. 269-74). Fletcher characterizes Lawrence as a "fine, intolerant fanatic."

[72] *Aaron's Rod.*

[73] The passages Lawrence cites are from throughout *Can Grande's Castle* (Boston, 1918). The "thunderheads marching along the skyline" first appear on page 3 of "Sea-Blue and Blood-Red," Lowell's recounting of the Lord Nelson-Lady Hamilton story. Venice is the "beautiful, faded city" (p. 171) in "The Bronze Horses," and the "fifty vessels . . . blowing up the Bosphorus" (p. 155) are from the same piece. The "English Coaches" are a major motif in "Hedge Island," an evocation of the old England. It is peculiar that the splashy, colorful, impressionistic "polyphonic prose" of *Can Grande's Castle* leads Lawrence to suggest that Lowell should write a play.

74 *Touch and Go.*

75 "What do I care!" "Sage" means "well-behaved" (said of a child). Lawrence may be playing with "sagesse," which means both good behavior and worldly wisdom.

76 Edgar Jaffe (1865-1921) was married to but separated from Frieda's older sister Else. An academic and economist, he was Minister of Finance in Kurt Eisner's short-lived People's Republic of Bavaria. Jaffe appears as Alfred Kramer in *Mr. Noon.* Hartmann von Richthofen (1878-1953) was a National Liberal politician who supported the peace resolution that passed in the Reichstag in July 1917.

77 Lawrence is correct: the Castel Vecchio in Verona was built by Cangrande II, a della Scala, in 1354. Lowell takes the phrase "Can Grande's castle" from "At the British Museum," a poem by Richard Aldington.

78 Of *New Poems.*

79 *Bay,* published in November 1919.

80 The review originally appeared in the *New York Times Review of Books* for 20 April 1919, pp. 205, 210-11, 215, 217. This review is collected in *Poetry and Poets,* edited by Ferris Greenslet and published in 1930.

81 Gilbert Cannan, John Davys Beresford, and Compton Mackenzie were popular English novelists. Lawrence became friendly with Cannan and Mackenzie when they were all neighbors in Buckinghamshire in the summer of 1914. Cf. Lawrence's letter to Lowell, 13 February 1920, Letter 49.

82 As it turned out, the Lawrences did not arrive in America until September 1922.

83 Gibson is remembered as a Georgian, though he lived until 1962. His long lecture tour in the United States in 1917 included three months in Chicago.

84 Understandably concerned about how Lawrence would respond to this letter, Lowell immediately wrote Frieda a letter asking her assistance in making "him understand that I only write this to help him." Cf. Letter 92.

85 *Pictures of the Floating World.*

86 In the summer of 1916 in New Hampshire, Lowell and Ada Russell were returning from an afternoon ride in Lowell's rig when a storm blew up. The horse panicked and went the wrong direction, and when Lowell yanked the reins sharply to turn the mare around, the buggy wound up with its wheels stuck in the mud of a shallow ditch. Lowell handed the reins to Russell and got out and lifted the back end of the buggy onto the road again. She tore some muscles and started the

umbilical hernia that was at last to kill her. The operation she mentions to Lawrence took place on 10 February 1920.

[87] Cannan's brief essay, "A Defense of Lawrence," had appeared in the *New York Tribune*, 10 January 1920. In it he praised Lawrence as "a man of genius and a person of vital importance to the intellectual and imaginative life of our time."

[88] The first edition, bound in paper wrappers, had appeared in 1918.

[89] Cyril Beaumont, a London bookseller, created the Beaumont Press, which issued new books of poetry in a handsome, expensive format. *Bay* was the eighth title in the series.

[90] In his postcard of 26 November 1919, Lawrence had reported that "there is still some blessed *insouciance* in the Italians." Cf. Letter 47.

[91] *The Lost Girl.* Lawrence had begun the novel in 1913 but left it in Germany before the outbreak of World War I. The manuscript caught up with Lawrence in Capri in February 1920, but after trying to continue it, he scrapped it and started over.

[92] "But one must take the rough with the smooth."

[93] Baylor University, celebrating its Diamond Jubilee, conferred fifty-six honorary Litt. D.'s. Lowell, Edwin Markham, Vachel Lindsay, Judd Mortimer Lewis, and Harriet Monroe were the poets honored.

[94] "Rondeau of a Conscientious Objector," "Nostalgia," and "Obsequial Chant" had appeared in *Voices* for July 1919.

[95] "Souvenir."

[96] Seltzer's *Women in Love*, privately printed for subscribers, was issued in November 1920. The Secker edition, published the following June, has many textual differences. Secker did not publish an edition of *The Rainbow* until 1926. *The Lost Girl* was never serialized.

[97] *Touch and Go.*

[98] "A real peasant girl."

[99] This review, entitled "A Voice Cries in Our Wilderness," was printed in the *New York Times* on 22 August 1920. The review was reprinted in *Poetry and Poets.*

[100] Scofield Thayer had purchased the *Dial* in December 1919.

[101] Mountsier was Lawrence's American agent between 1920 and 1923.

[102] *Birds, Beasts and Flowers.*

[103] North.

[104] Florence Wheelock Ayscough was an old friend who had become an expert on China. Lowell and Ayscough collaborated on the translations of ancient Chinese poems published in *Fir-Flower Tablets* in December 1921. There is evidence that Lowell saw herself as competing with Pound's poems after the Chinese.

[105] "Mosquito" appeared in the American *Bookman* for July 1921 (Volume 53, pp. 430-31). Lowell's review is found on pp. 404-06 of the same magazine. Lawrence's "Apostolic Beasts" appeared in the *Dial* for April 1921 (Volume 70), pp. 410-16.

[106] Mary M. Colum's review, entitled "The Quality of Mr. D. H. Lawrence," appeared in the *Freeman* of 22 June 1921 (Volume 6, pp. 357-8).

[107] The actual titles of the poems from *Legends* that Lawrence refers to are "Many Swans," "Funeral Song for the Indian Chief Blackbird," "Witch-Woman," "The Statue in the Garden," "Memorandum Confided by a Yucca to a Passion-Vine," and "A Legend of Porcelain."

[108] "Whitman" appeared in the *Nation and Athenaeum* for 23 July 1921 (Volume 29, pp. 616-18).

[109] *Birds, Beasts and Flowers* was not published until October 1923.

[110] "This trouble must end."

[111] "So much the worse for her!"

[112] "Never again."

[113] This work was published as *Fantasia of the Unconscious* in October 1922.

[114] "Where to?"

[115] "Affectionate greetings."

[116] Lawrence was awarded the James Tait Black Memorial Prize and £100 late in 1921 for the best English novel of 1920. This was the only official recognition he received for his writing during his lifetime.

[117] The eight paintings used to illustrate the book were done by Jan Juta, a young South African whom Lawrence knew in Italy.

[118] *Fir-Flower Tablets*, the collaboration with Florence Ayscough.

[119] It was Mabel Dodge Sterne, wealthy collector of writers and artists, who invited Lawrence to Taos.

[120] On 7 July 1922 the New York Society for the Suppression of Vice raided the offices of Thomas Seltzer, Lawrence's American publisher at the time, and confiscated all the copies of *Women in Love, A Young Girl's Diary*, and *Casanova's Homecoming*. Seltzer was charged with selling obscene literature. The case was dismissed on 12 September with the judge finding that each of the three books was "a distinct contribution to the literature of the day." (Lawrence, *Letters to Thomas and Adele Seltzer*, ed. Gerald M. Lacy, Black Sparrow Press, 1976, p. 184.) Cf. Lawrence's letter of 19 October 1922, Letter 73, in which he reports that Seltzer won his case.

[121] "As for the others, I don't give a damn."

[122] Henry James Forman's "With D. H. Lawrence in Sicily" appeared

in the *New York Times Book Review and Magazine* for 27 August 1922, p. 12. Forman, who had been a journalist, was a professional writer. His short essay on Lawrence is reprinted in Volume II of *D. H. Lawrence: A Composite Biography*, ed. Edward Nehls (Madison: University of Wisconsin Press, 1958), pp. 104-09.

[123] As Associate Editor of *Poetry*, Alice Corbin Henderson was not always sympathetic to Lowell's poetry. Bynner had been one of the perpetrators of the "Spectric" school of contemporary poetry, a hoax parodying Imagism and other new poetic schools of the World War I period.

[124] Sergeant was also a writer. Her sympathetic "Portrait" of Lowell is collected in *Fire Under the Andes: A Group of North American Portraits* (Knopf, 1927).

[125] Lawrence crossed out two false starts before sticking with "Mahomet."

[126] "The Evening Land" and "Turkey-Cock."

[127] Lawrence closes this letter with an exuberant curvilinear scrawl rather than a complimentary close.

[128] The article is "Taos," published in the *Dial* for March 1923 (Volume 74, pp. 251-54).

[129] Frieda responded to this letter on 14 August 1923. Cf. Letter 93.

[130] "Days gone by! Too long gone by!"

[131] *The Plumed Serpent.*

[132] "Until then!"

[133] Again an exuberant curvilinear scrawl instead of a complimentary close.

[134] "Greetings and remembrances."

[135] Amy Lowell died on 12 May 1925.

[136] *Aaron's Rod.*

[137] The correct date is 1885.

[138] Frieda is probably remembering the fact that Lawrence received his teacher's certificate in 1908 with distinctions in Maths, History and Geography, French, and Botany, but not in English.

Printed September 1985 in Santa Barbara & Ann Arbor
for the Black Sparrow Press by Graham Mackintosh
& Edwards Brothers Inc. Design by Barbara Martin.
There are 500 hardcover trade copies; 100 hardcover
copies have been numbered & signed by the editors;
& 26 copies handbound in boards by Earle Gray have
been lettered & signed by the editors.

E. Claire Healey is Professor of English at Montclair State College. She has published essays on Amy Lowell, Pound, and H.D. She is currently editing the correspondence between Lowell and H.D.

Keith Cushman is Professor of English at the University of North Carolina at Greensboro and President-Elect of the D. H. Lawrence Society of North America. He is the author of *D. H. Lawrence at Work*. His many published essays include studies of Lawrence, Joyce, Kafka, Fitzgerald, Beckett, Ted Hughes, Philip Larkin, Anais Nin, Bellow, Philip Roth, and Joyce Carol Oates. He is currently writing a book on Lawrence and his friends the Brewsters.